MEMORIES OF HELL, VISIONS OF HEAVEN

A Story of Survival, Transformation and Hope

Esther Joseph

ISBN: 1-4664-9749-1
ISBN-13:   9781466497498

Acknowledgements

Darota
Denise
Margarita
Val
Victoria
I bow to each and everyone of you, my sisters!

Contents

DEDICATION

To my soul family
who gave me my story and the voice to share it.

And to
Adela and Declan, your generous spirit inspired me.

Part I

MEMORIES

Introduction

I am sitting at the kitchen table of my childhood Saint Lucian home writing a letter. Bridges, my white German shepherd mix, is lying behind me making a strange whiny sound. He is smart, and knows how to push my buttons. I spoil him always giving in to whatever he wants, the moment he wants them. I repeatedly ask him to stop making that annoying sound, but he does not obey.

In anger and frustration, I turn around and hit him on the nose with the pen I am using —its point upwards. The pen pierces his right eye, injuring it. Realizing what I have done, I quickly run to the kitchen sink, grab a towel, soak it in cold water, and place it on his injured eye. But Bridges recoils, whimpering, rubbing his watery, wounded eye. I start crying uncontrollably.

"Oh, my God! Bridges! What have I done? I am *sooo* sorry! Please, God, stop his pain and restore his sight!" I begged.

Waking from the disturbing dream, I remained in bed sobbing, wondering what it meant. I could not imagine myself hurting my beloved Bridges. How could I abuse my closest companion of fourteen years? As a puppy, Bridges helped save me from self-destruction. He is the son I never had.

Bridges is part of my present life, but in the dream, we were in my childhood home, a place I had not lived for over thirty years. I was realizing that my past was the key to unlocking the full meaning of this nightmare. Moreover, it confirmed something I have known most of my adult life. Whether victim or perpetrator, abuse is a learned behavior, which becomes a part of you, as though it is in your genes.

Right there still lying in that bed, it became clear.

The avenue to ending the stranglehold of my past was in sharing my story. That would be my catalyst to peace.

If I could show you, dear reader, that the pattern of violence does not remain hidden in the past, but repeated like a scratched CD in the brain of both the abused and abuser, poisoning every facet of their lives, then my suffering would not be in vain and I could finally let it go. Before this revelation, I would never have considered this arduous undertaking. I found nothing appealing about divulging my darkest secrets and most unflattering qualities. Only such an awaking dream could have ignited this course of action.

While writing the book I discovered how disturbingly common my story is. Child abuse is out of control, the statistics flabbergasting. I knew it was a problem, yet overwhelmed by all the facts that made my assumptions more concrete. Childhelp, a national non-profit organization indicates that, "14% of men and 36% of women in prison in the USA were victims of abuse. Children who experience child abuse and neglect are 59% more likely arrested as a juvenile; 28% likely arrested as an adult; and 30% more likely to commit violent crimes. Teen pregnancy is 25% **more likely among victims; 60% of people in drug rehab centers report being abused as a child; and about 30% of abused children will later abuse their own children, continuing the cycle.**

My prayer dear friend is that my experience and journey of recovery will serve as hope to you if affected by this affliction. In that spirit I offer simple but concrete steps that will help alter your course and set you on the solid foundation of change you seek. Know this, no matter your past, it does not define you, nor determine your future. For I am persuaded that you, like me, can break the bonds of your past and find your way to the future and life you crave.

Christmas Princess

I AWOKE TO THE sounds of loud voices and the clanking of pots and pans. Slowly, I stretched, rubbing fists against sleepy eyes and was about to turn over, pull the tattered covers over my head and return to sleep, when my eyes popped open and a warm tingly feeling filled my slight body. It's Christmas!

I jumped out of bed, put my rag bedding away and slipped into my dress, an oversized t-shirt, the same soiled one I had worn the day before, and hurried to the only bedroom window. My father was outside; I can tell he had been up all night, busily cleaning and cutting the cow and goat meat gathered from the animals he had butchered. My mother and two older sisters, Elizabeth and Francisca, were in the outside kitchen, seasoning and cooking the meat. My mother looked up and saw me at the window. With both hands still buried in the container of meat she was seasoning, yelled, "Go get me more celery and parsley from the garden!"

"Yes, Mom!" I called back excitedly, as I ran out the back door. Our garden consisted of a number of long rows of various herbs, with walking pathways between them. Planted were basil, celery, cilantro, mint, and much more. At seven years old, I was getting very good at identifying most of the herbs and enjoyed helping with the planting and picking. And finally now assist with the cooking.

I picked a handful of the herbs my mom wanted, and since mint was my favorite, I grabbed a handful of that too. I took a moment to dally and inhale the fresh scents that filled the morning breeze; the combined aromas stirred all my senses.

I loved our majestic Caribbean isle, Saint Lucia, captivated by her vastness and magnificence. I took pleasure in the colors and greenery of my families' assorted gardens, the loveliness of the massive trees stretching far beyond them, and the mountains that provided a picture-perfect backdrop.

Produce from our other gardens included: cucumbers, lettuce, tomatoes, watermelon pumpkin and a variety of peppers. Huge mango and tangerine trees surrounded our house and the gardens, as did a display of colorful wildflowers. One of the tangerine trees was so close to our house that my siblings and I could pick the fruit from our bedroom door. Even further out, we grew bananas, coconuts, papayas, and more mangos. Our section of land was part of an even bigger area of property shared by our family, my mother's brothers and sisters, and their families. My two uncles, Gregra and Sonny Boy, grew other kinds of fruits and vegetables in their fields. Oranges and soursops made them lots of money. Many of us neighborhood kids often grabbed oranges from their trees. They hated it and complained often to our parents.

"Hurry up!" Elizabeth hollered. So I rushed to the kitchen with the herbs.

My family *prepared all year* for this one day. Aside from Christmas being a religious celebration, we also celebrated my godparents' yearly visit. Friendship aside, my godparents were rich, so my father always wanted to impress them.

The house would be fitted with brand new lanolin carpets, new curtains, and a holiday-decorated plastic tablecloth for the only living room table. And if my father had managed to save enough money, a fresh coat of paint. On Christmas Day, the Joseph family had more to eat and drink than on any other day of the entire year. On Christmas, we were rich!

I slept on the wooden floor of a tiny bedroom with my three older sisters, while the living room became my four brothers' bedroom. Our "beds" were sugar and flour sacks as a base, then covered with layers of old clothes and rags, which we laid out every night, then picked up and stuffed into the sacks, and hid away in the morning. Once a week, my sisters washed all the bedding. On top of supplying the water needed for the washing, I helped hang the pieces of cloth on a line tied between two trees or drape them on stones to dry in the sun. Sleeping on old rags may seem lumpy and uncomfortable, but to us, it was our version of a bed and all we knew.

We certainly were not the only family who lived that way; most families living in the countryside, could not afford modern conveniences and appliances. Running water, indoor plumbing, and gas or electric stoves were rich city folk luxuries. We had outhouses and outdoor kitchens.

Our outdoor kitchen, a crude, shaky structure, made of four thin posts holding up a few galvanized sheets that served as a roof had a fire pit made of three large stones, where a black cooking pot sat. Below the pot, large chunks of burning wood formed huge, smoky black flames that slow-cooked our ground provisions: sweet potatoes, yams, green plantains, and bananas. My brothers were in charge of collecting, chopping, and feeding the wood to the fire while the women cooked. We also had a small indoor eating area, which had a charcoal pit, used on rainy days or to cook breakfast, meat, and fish—things easier and faster to cook.

On a regular day, if I'd looked towards that outdoor kitchen, only one fire pit would be going, if any; but on that Christmas morning, I gasped at the spectacular sight and smell of three big bubbling pots. Yum!

In addition to being rich and living in Castries, Saint Lucia's capital and only city, my godparents were cool, always laughing and having a good time. Of Eastern Indian decent, my godfather was the handsomest man I knew, with perfect brown skin, wavy black hair, and trimmed sideburns. During his visits, he wore his shirt with too many top buttons undone. Our eyes were instantly drawn to the cross hanging from the gold chain nestled in the dark hairs on his chest. His shirt tucked into his trousers all held together with a shiny belt.

My godmother, Maylia, also of Eastern Indian decent, was pretty and petite. Her black hair was so long and straight she could wear it in three styles: pinned in a tight bun, ponytail or flowing loosely down to her butt. On that occasion, she wore it in a single braided ponytail. She was the only person I knew who wore high heels. The points of her heels were so sharp that they poked holes in my mother's brand new carpets. After the celebration, my siblings and I would count all the holes her sharp heels had left behind. We could track her movements by following the holes. My mother would shake her head in wonder and ask, "How can she do it, how can she keep these things on all day and look so comfortable?" and did not mind that my godmother had damaged her new carpets.

Together with all the delicious food, drinks, and new decorations, my godparents were the best thing about Christmas. Their big car in front of our house told everyone the party is on, so our neighbors and friends, including Ms. Janie my mother's best friend and her family, joined in. My godparents loved to dance—especially my godfather, who loved Merengue. He always started the party by dancing, usually with a drink in hand, he always danced with his wife first, spinning her around and planting exaggerated kisses on her cheek, impressing everyone with his fancy dance moves. "Isn't she beautiful?" he would say.

As Maylia's wide skirt billowed and swirled, my godfather would compliment her dancing and tell her how nice she looked. When she finally needed to rest her high-heeled feet, he'd ask the next available woman to dance. He would dance with my mother and sisters, saying nice things to each one, making them feel special too.

Not having a partner did not keep my godfather off the dance floor. He'd simply raise a hand above his head, wrap the other around his stomach, and did the Caribbean "wine and wiggle" with his waist and hips. When he got tired of dancing with himself, he would pull someone— anyone–onto the dance floor with him.

I cherished the moments he danced with me. "Come, princess!" he'd say, holding out his hand. Placing my small bare feet on his glossy shoes, he would hold me close as we twirled to the music. "My, my, you get prettier every time I set eyes on you, young lady, and so grown up too. I bet you are the smartest one in your class. Am I right?" I'd giggle with pride and delight. At the end of our dance, he always gave me money. That Christmas he gave me a lot. Five dollars! "Buy whatever you want," he whispered with a wink. One day a year, I was a happy princess. Dancing on my godfather's big strong feet was where my lifelong love for dance and music began.

I spent most of my days wishing my godparents were my real parents and wondering how people so different could be friends. Unlike my father, the more my godfather drank the livelier and more fun he became. He was never disrespectful, even in a drunken state. People gravitated towards him, while they simply tolerated my father.

I prayed often that someday my godparents would come take me away to live with them. I imagined myself running around their yard, eating delicious desserts from their ice cream maker, and sleeping in my own room in their huge house in the city. There, I would have beautiful things that belonged only to me, no hand-me-downs. I would not have to share a single thing with anyone. I knew that at my godparents' house, every day would be like Christmas!

After the celebration and the last drunken, prolonged "bon fet, an nou fe anko lana pwochen" (Great party! Let's do it again next year) echoed, came the part I dreaded. All day long, my father had been friendly—the perfect host—but as soon as the guests were gone and we were in bed, comatose and anxious for sleep, he became a different person. From our room, we could easily hear him nitpicking at everything he felt my mother had done incorrectly: a dish had not been prepared to his liking, or she had said something he felt was inappropriate, using them as reasons to start a fight with her. Usually it began with an inflated clearing of his throat, followed by a slight pause, and then his signature phrase, "yes...yes...yes...aha" "pou kisa ou vle fem mwan fasche? Gade mwan, gade!" (Why you want to make me angry? Look at me, look!) . Not a sound from my mother.

"I don't want to be mad at you, but you make me. Why do you have to make me mad? Why? Why do you always do that? You make me look bad, with all my friends!" As he slapped his palms together, he'd reprimand. "You still don't know how to stew meat? After all this time, you cannot do anything right! "Mova famn...malpwop madamn!" ("Bad wife...nasty woman!")

The more he taunted, the angrier and louder he got, curse words shooting out like from the muzzle of a shotgun.

"You just can't keep your frickin' fat mouth shut. You go around telling the whole goddamn world how much this cost that costs. Salop! It's my money, my business. Not yours, mine! You hear me?"

This would go on for hours, accompanied by a thumping chest, headboard, anything he could get his hands on. My mother would lie next to him, silent, hoping and praying I imagine that he'd fall asleep or keep the onslaught verbal. But, at some point during the night, he would start pounding on her too. Her screams would jolt us out of bed as he starts beating her mercilessly. My siblings would rush into their bedroom to help her, and the evening would turn into an all-night battle between my father and siblings, ensuring that no one would be getting any sleep. Whether an ordinary day, holiday or family outing, whenever he was drank, my father would turn our days into nightmares that always ended in bloodshed as he tried to defend himself against the fury of his children.

One drizzling weekday morning, Elizabeth informed me that I would not be going to school that day. When I asked why, she merely said, "You won't understand."

I could tell that my mother had been crying and everyone was unusually quiet. A few neighbors, including Ms. Janie, dropped by, after brief exchanges they stood around in puzzled silence, as if there was something they too did not understand.

That afternoon, Elizabeth dressed me in my favorite outfit, a pink dress with a golden ribbon running down the front. I followed my parent's example and remained silent throughout the long bus ride to the big stone church in the city square. Sadness was everywhere. Most people, especially my godmother, were sobbing and wailing nonstop. I wondered why people had to help her walk. It frightened me to see her so upset. I kept looking around for my godfather. I knew that as soon as he showed up, he would make her laugh and smile again, but he was gone.

I was about eight years old when my godfather passed away suddenly at the young age of forty. I never knew my godfather's real name until recently; I found it on my birth certificate. To me, he was my Artoe. I still think of him, and cherish the memory of dancing on my Artoe's feet, and being someone's princess. My last dance with Mr. Patrick Butcher was the last time I experienced the happiness of feeling truly loved.

After my godfather died, there were fewer celebrations at my house. My father became less interested and involved in Christmas. It got to the point where he claimed my mother was spending too much of *his* money on food and decorations, so these things were slowly toned down and eventually disappeared altogether.

Religion in the Mix

PERHAPS IT WAS THE untimely death of my godfather that caused my mother to start thinking about her mortality. The Jehovah's Witnesses, Seventh Day Adventists, and Pentecostals came around often to "witness" and compete for her soul. The Pentecostals won out, she accepted Jesus as her Savior, got water baptized, and became a Born-again Christian. My mother chose to convert to Pentecostal because of that religion's belief that God takes care of the problems of those who believe in him. When she died she would go to heaven, a place where milk and honey flowed, sealed the deal.

The prospect of having a better life, eventually, enticed her. It did not matter that she would have to die before she could enjoy it. She probably assumed she'd have an early death at the hands of her husband anyway, so heaven wasn't too far off. They promised that if she asked God to save her from her wretched life of sin, she could lay all her troubles in his almighty hands. Up to then, no one had been able to help her, so it sounded like that new God would finally lend a hand. One of my mother's favorite hymns, which she sang for years, expressed her new conviction: "Because he lives I can face tomorrow, because he lives all fear is gone, because I know he holds the future and life is worth the living just because he lives."

Prior to this point, my mother drank alcohol and danced socially, but now these were sinful acts according to her new Pentecostal philosophy. After becoming a Christian, she no longer partook in those pleasures of the flesh, practices my father thoroughly enjoyed. This really didn't help her case.

A good Pentecostal attended church every Sunday and participate in many other church gatherings. This included weekly prayer meetings, Bible study classes, and women group services.

My mother found comfort in her religion and enjoyed going to the meetings. It gave her purpose and something to look forward to, but gave my father new reasons to make her life even more intolerable. He resented the time she spent away from home, and her continuous singing and cheerfulness annoyed him further. Accordingly, the fighting at home was more frequent and intense. My poor mother just could not win.

Her favorite service was the prayer meeting on Wednesday nights. She made an extra effort to get her chores done quickly to get herself ready for the evening. She'd walk the two miles to the church cheerfully, probably singing all the way, with hope in her heart and pep in her step. But my father was quick to figure out her new evening schedule, and began his threatening tirades on Monday evenings in bed.

"I'm putting you on notice! That prayer thing, don't even think about it! You spend *all* your frickin' time in that frickin' church. Something wrong with you, woman?" His voice would get louder and angrier, "what the hell is going on here, you spend your time doing everything but taking care of *my* business in *my* house, anymore." The few times my mother did try to answer back, the fighting only escalated. She learned that not responding was the best way to save her skin and neck.

"You think I don't see? You think I don't know? Oh, I know. You think I'm stupid? No. I see everything! I know everything! I know you giving *my* money and *my* food to that fat-ass lazy preacher man! All your talk is *Brother this* and *Sister that*. What the frickin hell is that anyway? I know you're sleeping with one of them over there. What frickin' Brother is it? Tell me! I'm putting you on notice right now! If you go, don't come back! I will sharpen my cutlass sharp, sharp—and *Mwen kai koupe tèt ou!* (I will chop off your head!). You hear me?"

Eventually, my mother reluctantly gave up her weeknight activities, but refused to give up the Sunday services, which entailed early Bible study and a very long congregational mass. The preaching would go on for hours!

Early Sunday mornings, she'd leave for church, dragging me with her. I would count the minutes until I could get out of there. I knew the repercussions waiting at home and regardless of how terrible my father's actions would be, I just wanted the ugly scene over as soon as possible.

We would return home starving around two or three in the afternoon. My father would be sitting in the kitchen looking out the window, fuming. Whether we entered the house quietly through the front or kitchen side door, he would see us. Sometimes, as my mother would be in her room changing her clothes, he would follow her there. Other times, the fighting started immediately.

Often, my father began by tossing out the food my mother prepared that morning before church, and we would have no lunch. Another precious meal wasted, my belly grumbled from hunger as my body pined for nourishment, but mostly my mind yearned for some peace.

"If you think I'm going to eat this cold, salty pile of crap that's been sitting out here all day, you're crazy, woman! You have another thing coming," he'd shout, hurling the pot out the window.

Sunday is considered a holy day of rest, but at our house, it was the unholiest of days. The consequences of my mother spending a few hours at church became a weeklong war between my father, my mother, and my oldest siblings.

One particular Sunday afternoon, after a long and vicious fight between the adults, the situation finally cooled down, my siblings left the house to recuperate and distance themselves from our father.

About half an hour after they left, I was sitting outside trying to escape the tension inside the house. Suddenly, my mother darted out the kitchen door and into the fields in the back of the house. She kept checking to see if my father was chasing her. She was running at top speed while looking back at the same time, that she slammed into the trunk of a huge breadfruit tree. The impact was so intense that she fell heavily to the ground, the wind knocked out of her. She was obviously hurt.

I ran to her and, although it could've been the shock and the pain of the moment, I could see a change in her face as she sat there for a while gathering herself.

Eventually, she got up, unsteadily. I had never seen her with that look before; it was more than just rage and determination. She picked up a large rock and purposefully, single-mindedly, moved towards the house. My father, in his usual spot at the kitchen table gazing out the window, did not see her approaching. My mother planted herself outside the kitchen door a few feet away from him and tossed the rock at his head. She missed; the stone simply crushed through the thin plywood kitchen wall, puncturing a huge hole between the kitchen and living room. The gap in the wall was never repaired. It remained to bear witness to my mother's only solo attempt at defending herself.

My father barely reacted; he probably chuckled inside. He must have been shocked that she did anything at all, but I could not tell from his unchanged expression. He merely got up from his chair, meandered out the house through the front door, up the hill towards the rum shops.

My mother's tree-crashing incident caused her great injury, physical pain, and internal bleeding. For about a week after, she was spitting up blood and spend days in bed drinking homemade remedies to recover. Of course, my father didn't care.

I remember this particular incident because I never understood why my mother did not ever try to defend herself before. She assumed and said as much, there was no chance of ever escaping my father. His unfailing threats and ill-treatment made her believe that she had no choice. Nevertheless, I know that my mother could have easily killed my father and gotten away with it. The whole community was well aware that she had every reason to do so, and some people even suggested it. "Why don't you just kill the bastard and get it over with?" they would say, especially the women.

My mother was forever crying and suffered countless broken bones at the hands of my father. Her frequent black eyes, cut swollen lips, scrapes and bruises were unmistakable evidence that gave her the right to avenge herself.

Meet the Folks

LIONEL JOSEPH, MY FATHER, was really a mild-mannered hard-working farmer. He never quarreled or got into brawls with his fellow drinkers at the rum shops, but rather saved the adrenalin the liquor produced for when he got home. Everything my father did the money he earned, the actions he took, were all a prelude to getting drunk and wreaking havoc in our lives. Alcohol fueled the anger, hatred, and bitterness, he directed toward his family, especially his wife.

My mother Suzanna, had her first child at nineteen, and married my father, four years her senior, when she was twenty-three years old. She has a nice wide smile, although I rarely saw her smiling. I used to enjoy watching my mother dance with my godfather at our Christmas celebrations, but I don't remember ever seeing her dance with my father.

My mother was a good cook, but with time she become so nervous while cooking that she would over-salt or overcook our meals. Afraid of her own shadow, she got so jittery that, over the years, developed a nervous twitch. I was about eleven when I learned of my mother's little habit.

I was on the playground one day after school when an angry classmate I had just beaten as term leader at a game of Rounders, a combination of baseball and dodge ball, called my entire family stupid cheaters. She went on, flapping her eyes for effective dramatization, "Your mother is such a stupid retard! She can't stop blinking!" Flapping her eyes some more.

"You fat liar!" I screamed, shoving her to the ground.

I run all the way home that day and went straight into the kitchen where my mother stood cooking at the coal pit stove. Standing inches from her, I gazed directly and unflinchingly into her face. She continued stirring the pot of chicken she was stewing for dinner, tasting the gravy for flavor. Finally, I noticed what everyone else knew. My mother was indeed a serial blinker!

Gilbert was the first child. We referred to each other as Alpha and Omega—the beginning and the end. In the looks department, our parents blessed Gilbert with all that was fine. The women loved him and he loved them all back.

Everything about Gilbert was black, so he was nicknamed "Black," which he liked and carried with pride. His perfect white teeth made his blackness even more pronounced, although eventually he lost almost all of them to his many dance hall and street fights. He wore his curly jet-black hair in a huge afro, with an afro comb sticking out of it. Slim and fit, with an easy roaring laugh.

He was my savior and knight, but his armor was far from shiny. He fought and argued everywhere he went - even with the police. Often, we would find out about his arrest the next day from a neighbor or from whomever he had assaulted the night before.

When he was in his early thirties, Gilbert became a Rastafarian and moved to the wilderness. He gave up all communication with the outside world, including us. Occasionally, my brothers would see him when they went out that far into the forest, but he made a point of ignoring them. The rest of the family did not see him for years.

Joseph arrived next. I heard that our parents and his godparents were so drunk at his baptism that they christened him Joseph Joseph. Poor Joseph! It does not take much for kids to tease each other, and my brother just could not avoid being the brunt of their hurtful jokes. "Your parents couldn't think of a name for you so they gave you the same one twice? That's so dumb!" They'd say.

As Joseph grew older, his name became more of an inconvenience. Since his name seemed like a typo, the confusion caused delayed or returned paperwork. When he became an adult, he legally had it changed to Alexander.

He was the opposite of Gilbert, and they did not get along. I think they secretly envied each other, admiring the qualities they saw in one another, that they thought they lacked within themselves. While Gilbert did not have a problem taking on our father and actually seemed to relish in it, Joseph was terrified of him. Whenever our father addressed him, Joseph would inexplicably start to stutter. For a while, he took part in trying to defend our mother against our father, but the older he got, the more often he would vanish when the fighting began. He would head into the back-fields, and I imagine he slept out there because we would not see him until morning.

Joseph's inabilities to stand up to our father made him feel small and Gilbert delighted in reminding him, "Where did you run off to last night, little man? Someday you'll have to get that tail out of your ass or I'll have to do it for you myself!"

The older he got, the more Joseph withdrew. Exceptionally moody he did not have many friends. Joseph kept his feelings bottled up inside, allowing his anger from past grievances to build and fester. When Gilbert teased or belittled him, or when one of us had any disagreements with him, Joseph would not react but simply walked away. No one would realize how deeply upset he was or had been, until his anger would suddenly explode in shrill regurgitations of incomprehensible words and rumblings. We would have to piece together his words to figure out what he was saying, as he'd replay a previous incident when someone had offended him. Clenched fists, foaming at the mouth, glazed, bulging eyes Joseph reminded me of a crazed caged animal. He would tremble as if he was an erupting volcano about to burst. Usually these episodes ended as quickly and as suddenly as they started. His unpredictability frightened everyone, including our mother. He had this certain stabbing stare—filled with hatred and disgust. I was petrified of him.

Our family practiced a hands-off approach when it came to Joseph. In his teens, he had a psychotic break and taken to a mental institution. My family has never spoken openly about this; however, after his first visit to the institution, the doctor's instructions were discussed in hushed whispers. The doctors recommended that Joseph keep away from all stress, particularly our chaotic home environment, diagnosed as the cause of his breakdown. The adults were considering sending him away to live with another family, but that never happened. My father, on the other hand, did what he did best: ignored his family needs claiming it was Joseph's problem not his.

Joseph was one of my mother's favorites. She felt great grief and guilt at having contributed to his illness and became a passionate defender of his strange behavior and lack of interest or involvement in family affairs.

Joseph later got married and had four children, but sadly went on to treating his family with the same quiet distain he did us. It came as no surprise to me that at the age of fifty-one, Joseph passed away from a variety of different cancers that had eaten him up inside. At the end, I was heartbroken that we had not taken the opportunity to get to know each other.

Elizabeth, the third and oldest daughter, resembles and acts the most like our mother, and the first of my siblings to follow our mother into Pentecostalism. As the oldest daughter, she cared for us when our mother was away selling crops at the city market, or seeking temporary refuge with family or friends when trying to get away from our father. All Elizabeth wanted was to make her big escape; her ticket out was marriage.

She never let us forget how much of a pain taking care of us was and released her frustrations by spanking the hell out of us. The smallest infraction would throw her into a fit of rage. She hated disobedience. Her so-called spankings turned into violent fights between her and the siblings who could stand up to her. I was not one of them.

In those days, children had absolutely no rights and spanking as punishment—at home and school—was acceptable and routine. In schools, paddles and belts were used to hit kids all over the body. Rulers on the knuckle and the ever-popular twists of the ear were effective in keeping students in line. However, what went on at my house went far beyond the spanking category. No matter how harmless the infraction, the level of punishment was an attempt to maim or kill you. At my house, the punishment was always disproportionate to the crime.

Nothing was off limits to Elizabeth, but her weapon of choice was her teeth. When her anger took over, Elizabeth turned into Dracula. When she laid her fangs on her prey, her bite marks on arms, necks, or legs left permanent scars.

One of my most memorable beatings was on the day I stole a nickel from her. Elizabeth, a seamstress, usually kept coins in her sewing machine drawer. One afternoon I wanted some candy, an instant-nasal-passage-clearing minty white sweetie we called *oh-so-strong*. It was my favorite. Tempted by the change in her drawer, I took a nickel when I thought no one was around. Either she knew exactly how much money she had in there or she saw me take it. But I was busted, literally.

She took her time delivering her punishment. She had me kneel, my knees bare on the uncarpeted, wooden living room floor, waiting for hours. She made a big production by telling everyone that I was a thief, making it seem like I was on my way to becoming a career criminal. She picked her punishing paraphernalia carefully, like a warrior choosing her weapons before stepping onto the battlefield. She made certain that she picked only items that would deliver the most pain—paddles, tree branches, and belts. She proceeded to use them one after another. Of the many beatings in my short lifetime, that was one of the worst.

After such beatings, I would make myself scarce. I would retreat to a neighbor's home or to a corner and take refuge in my thoughts. I fantasized about being part of another family, one in which parents and siblings treated each other with respect and were kind and compassionate to one another. In that family, there was no yelling or fighting, and everyone spoke in quiet, gentle tones. Some days I wished that I were an only child, other days I wish I had never been born, was dead, or artfully disappear. I was convinced no one would miss me if I did.

Our household daily chores were assigned according to age. Since we did not have running water, it was the responsibility of the youngest children to fetch water from the public water tap—a pump established by the government, which provided the entire village with its water supply. Our task was to fill two gigantic drums located on the outside of the house, so our older sisters would have water available for their tasks. Each drum had three indentations, and my two younger brothers and I had to fill both drums to the second indentation in order to meet the daily water requirements. That meant fetching water in the mornings and evenings on school days, and all day long on the weekends. We had to fill the drum to the brim on weekends because we watered all the crops and did more laundry during those days. Our failure to fill these drums was one of Elizabeth's greatest pet peeves.

The public tap was quite a distance away, or so it seemed for my skinny legs and arms carrying buckets of water in the sweltering heat. With time, we got so good at fetching water that we could balance a bucket on our heads and one in each hand, shortening the number of trips.

Easily distracted, I would often put down my buckets to chase or watch birds. If only I could grow wings like them, I thought, I would soar high above it all. I would fly to far away lands where no one would ever find me —ever. Taking to the air, I would devour all the yummy plump fruits and nuts growing at the tippy-top of the tall trees, living the high life.

On most days while journeying with the water, I would go sit in the fields surrounded by mangoes, coconuts, guavas, and other types of fruit trees. I liked climbing the tall mango trees to pick the fruits, while the guavas and plums were within my short reach. I was always hungry, and would sit and eat fruits in the warmth and comfort of the sun. Walking and balancing on the thick black pipes that carried the water into our area was an enjoyable distraction; these pipes were miles long. Eventually I would remember the reason for being out there in the first place and would run to gather the water. If I had really delayed Elizabeth from getting her work done on time, she would smack me. Sometimes it was worth it, though. My once-hungry tummy was now full of fresh juicy fruit and I had the pleasure of being in the peaceful outdoors away from her craziness for a little while.

My next oldest sister, Jeanette, was at one time my favorite. She was the first of all my siblings who had the initiative to make something of her life and moved to Castries to continue her education. Unlike the other young women her age, Jeanette was not waiting around for a man to support and take care of her. She attended the only vocational school in Saint Lucia, which offered a specialized agricultural business curriculum. A new and innovative college acceptance into the program was difficult. It was a proud moment for the family when she was accepted.

Jeanette had many friends and my only sister who went out on dates, or "gallivanting" as my parents liked to call it.

She rejected our mother's Pentecostal religion and became a very active member of the Catholic Church. Our mother resented it, as she felt Catholics were unsaved and called Jeanette a *jammet* (slut) destined for hell. My father hated the fact that Jeanette desired to educate herself. He accused her of being *pi ma ya* (arrogant or proud).

I admired Jeanette's ambition and independence. Not to mention, she always looked and smelled nice on her weekend visits. She was the one who beat up on me the least; sometimes she would even try to defend me, especially to our mother. When my mother complained about me to my siblings, Jeanette would remind her, "Well, that's normal, how kids behave." When I was a teenager, Jeanette even attempted to sway my mother to let me take dance classes, but there was no way my mother would allow me to do anything that would bring me joy.

Like all my siblings though, Jeanette had her dark side. She was obsessive and protective of her personal belongings: perfumes, clothes, and jewelry. From time to time, I would make use of her things, and no matter how careful I was in replacing the borrowed items, she would somehow always detect that someone had tampered with it.

When I was about ten or eleven years old, my body started to develop, even I was becoming aware of my body odor. Since my father barely provided enough money for food, luxury items like toothpaste, body lotions, and fragrant soaps were extravagances we could rarely afford. On the few occasions when we were able to purchase such products, they were gone as soon as they appeared. With little access to deodorants and soaps, Jeanette's fancy fragrances and body splashes were exactly what my body needed. They were irresistible!

On her return Friday evenings from her week at school and work, she would head directly to her corner of our bedroom. She would examine her dresser closely and knew instantly whether any of her items had been touched. Although she knew exactly who'd done it, she'd grant the courtesy of asking, "Who touched my stuff?" Since everyone knew who the culprit was, no one answered. She'd answer her own question by screaming, "Esta!" at the top of her lungs.

Most times, I would stick around and take my punishment. She would slap, punch, and kick me wildly. Covering my face was my only defense. If I had stained or spilled something, the punishment would be worse. On those occasions, I made myself scarce to delay the consequences, hoping she'd forget or leave on a date before I reappeared. During the beatings, I felt the emotional hurt more than the physical. How could my own sister care more about her possessions than for me, her little sister? I could not, and still cannot, comprehend why she would not want her baby sister to look and smell pretty as she did.

Francisca was my only sibling who played games with me. She was born to teach, but missed her calling. I credit her for my love of reading. She read to me when I was too young to comprehend, and we enjoyed playing reading games when I learned how to read. She volunteered at the school library, borrowing books she would entertain me for hours.

I learned that I could be smart and determined just like Nancy Drew— but it was the fairy tales that gave me hope that someone would someday come to save me. I, too, wanted to go to a party and have a prince return my lost slipper and take me away. Or, "let down my hair" like Rapunzel, allowing my hero to climb up to rescue me. These fantasies allowed me much-needed escape. For as long as I can remember, I've dreamt of being in other places, being another person, and live a life other than mine.

My favorite story was "Pinocchio". At the time, I didn't know why I liked it so much. Now I know that I related to him because I too yearned to be a boy. Life was much easier for my brothers. They had fun and freedom! I wanted anything, other than my life.

Francisca was a good daughter and favored by our mother. Timid and eager to please, she cleaned and decorated our broken-down house, making it as homey as possible. Her teen years were centered on the Pentecostal Church. She taught Sunday school classes and was devoted to them. Her commitment to the church always got her elected to many church leadership roles. Francisca and Elizabeth dressed in accordance with the church's protocol. Pentecostals, like most fundamentalist religions, expect the bodies of their female member's covered—long sleeves and long skirts— especially for church services. Women wore hats and veils to cover their hair. Dresses were loose fitting, not revealing cleavage or the contours of the body, especially the behind. Jewelry— except for wedding rings— makeup and pants were sins of vanity.

Our mother encouraged and was extremely proud of her girls. They delighted in talking and planning church activities together. When it came to the church, they were Jesus' three Musketeers.

Francisca was extremely responsible when it came to church, but there was one very puzzling thing about her. When our mother could not make it to the city on Saturdays, and it became Francisca's duty to travel to the city to purchase our groceries for the week, she would return hours later with no money and no food. She never had any explanations and refused to talk about it. No matter what questions were asked she'd repeat, "I don't know." When pressed for specifics, she would blow up into fits of rage and tears or sullen silence. My mother just chose to ignore the severity of the problem. The odd thing was that since my mother did not get mad at her, no one else did either. Our mother made excuses to our father as to why there wasn't sugar, rice or beans for that week.

One Saturday afternoon, Francisca returned home empty- handed again and stormed to our room before anyone could interrogate her. After a short while, I followed, and for a few minutes, we laid on the bedroom floor side by side in awkward silence. It must have been the combination of hunger and the disappointment over the absence of the fish we were expecting for dinner that prompted me to ask, "What happened? What did you do with the money?"

She did not answer. She merely turned her face away from me, but not before I saw the pain and confusion in her eyes. I am not sure what Francisca did with the money, but I believe the responsibility was just too much for her to handle. It was easy for her to be overwhelmed by the city marketplace and she was pick-pocketed or misplaced the money somehow. I know her actions were not malicious or intentional, but clearly, she was not the right person for the job. It took some time for my mother to realize that this had to stop, and passed the torch on to me. I was about twelve when I obtained the adult task of taking the bus to the city to purchase our weekly groceries. I believe Francisca's fervent faith and constant praying is what saved her from a fate similar to Joseph's mental state.

Lawrence's desire as a young man was to be as feared like our father and was my only sibling who consciously imitated him. He was defiant, vengeful, loved fighting, and did most of it at home. He bullied Elias and Francisca endlessly. I just stayed out of his way.

Pigheaded and irrational, it was impossible to reason with Lawrence, which meant every disagreement ended in a physical altercation. During his quarrels, he backed up his talk by always trying to find sharp objects.

During a confrontation with Lawrence, the aim was to keep him away from jagged objects, it case he would use them, even accidentally. It was more important to block or hide these objects from him than to throw or receive a blow.

Once, Lawrence and Francisca had a fierce encounter out in the fields where a pitchfork was involved. Lawrence was threatening Francisca with it, but she managed to grab and tossed it away. As they continued jabbing and pushing each other, Francisca accidently stepped on the pitchfork and was pierce in the foot. The sight of her own blood gave Francisca strength and further incentive to cause Lawrence to bleed also. Since Lawrence had to match her renewed vigor and elevated anger, the fighting only escalated. They were two wild beasts driven by the sight and smell of fresh blood. In the end, the screaming and shouting drew the attention of a neighboring farmer, who called our parents. Only then did the fighting stop.

Lawrence's toughest challenge was Elizabeth. When he did something deserving punishment, usually on a Saturday when our mother was away at the city market, Elizabeth would prepare, collecting necessary items: belts, paddles and sticks. She chose the safety of the kitchen, as it was made completely of wood, and broken glass could not become a weapon. Sealing the two windows and doors, she would also take the time to hide any other items he might try to use against her. Then Elizabeth would call or drag Lawrence into the kitchen. She would punish him with such fury, that ultimately, he would have to defend himself and the fracas would break out into a full-blown war. If Lawrence felt he had "won" a round, he'd come out proud and cocky. However, if wounded, he would emerge angrier and ready to provoke another fight—with someone weaker, of course.

Oh, Lawrence was mean. We were both born in the month of March, Lawrence on the third day, I was the ninth day. Our siblings would tease and annoy Lawrence by telling him that since the day I was born on was greater then the day he was born, then that made me older then him. Lawrence knew that I was not older then him, but could not quite make sense of how my greater birth date did not necessarily mean I was older. In his rage, and inability to understand, he would maliciously beat me up, even though all I had to do with it was share his birth month.

Although Elias was younger than Lawrence, Elias felt that as a boy, he should be able to defend himself. His technique in handling Lawrence was to not get him angrier. He would hit back in defense, but at the same time, try to talk Lawrence down. Elias would say things like "Stop it! Why you wanna hit me like that for? Come on, man, I didn't do anything to you!"

The fact that Elias was being reasonable and not challenging him often took the wind out of Lawrence's sails. Even so, he released his venom on Elias quite often. Their fights were more frequent, but shorter and less intense than Lawrence's fights with his sisters.

Elias was dishonest, gossipy, mischievous, and never owned up to his mistakes. When I was about ten years old, a neighbor who was our cousin, accused me of killing her chicken. I tried unsuccessfully to convince her and my sister Elizabeth that I had not killed the chicken. "How could you do this? How could you kill someone's chicken? Apologize right now to Miss Zeta!" Elizabeth kept shouting.

I insisted that, "I didn't do it." But my continued denial just made the embarrassing situation, and the whooping, worse.

Later, we discovered that Elias was the one who had stoned the chicken with his slingshot, and knowingly and cowardly stood by as I received punishment for his misdeed.

Elias was more feminine than I was his homemaking skills were far superior to mine. I was more interested in doing things outside the house. But Elias enjoyed household chores - considered women's work according to the mores of the time. The fact that he was adept at these things caused him grief. Lawrence liked calling him a "sissy," especially when they were among friends. Sometimes, when Lawrence and Elias were not fighting and actually playing, one of the games they played was "The Best Ways to Torture a Wife." They tried to come up with ideas on how they would torment their future wives and the one who came up with the most disturbing and creative affliction would be the winner. I remember listening once and hearing one of Elias's cruel fantasies, which involved trapping a woman in a tiny cage, starve and brand her with a hot iron, then inserting the iron up her butt. At the young ages of twelve and thirteen, they came to believe, that a woman's reason for being was to serve and be tortured by her man.

When Elias was nearly fourteen, he saved money and bought a bicycle—the first one owned by a Joseph child. Elias chained and locked his precious silver and black bicycle so I could not ride it—but I was a little Houdini and found a way to unlock the bike and rode it all over the neighborhood when he was away. I loved riding that bike, it made me feel strong and free, like a boy. It was the only time I felt as free as my brothers. Trying to relock the bike the same way was impossible, so I inevitability got busted.

At first, I begged. "Could I just ride it from here to there? I promise I won't scratch it." Pointing to a short distance, "Just a tiny, little minute, please...?" His reply was always the same: "No!" My only option was to borrow it on the sly. In the beginning, I was careful about keeping it clean and scratch-free—but after making use of it a few times, I wasn't as careful. I would ride farther and faster, and even race automobiles on the rugged unpaved roads. Riding this bike, I could feel the wind in my face and hair. It was the closest thing to having wings like a bird.

Freedom had a price though, when he returned home, Elias would make me pay. He loved punching me all over my body, and as soon as he discovered that girls' developing breasts were sensitive and should never be hit, he aimed for them. I became adept at protecting myself by crossing my arms over my chest while keeping my head down. Regardless, Elias was nothing compared to the others.

I was the annoying, inquisitive one who "why" everything and everyone to death. I made frequent use of the wide mouth and thick lips that engulfed my face. I took things that did not belong to me. At first I had no problem asking and saying please, but when refused what I wanted, I would respond with an "in your face" manner. I didn't have the physical strength to fight; but I had words and an attitude, which I amplified for maximum impact.

When my mother was lecturing about something she learned in church, I couldn't help but remind her of something she had done recently.

"Mom isn't giving Pastor Delease money and food, behind Daddy's back, dishonest? He tells you not to do it *all* the time, but you do it anyway."

"Shut your big mouth! I'm your mother, if I tell you to do something, you just do it!"

One day, the women from the various parishes came together to plan an upcoming social. My mother and some of the women were sitting on the floor chatting and laughing. I was sitting in the corner behind them, to the side of my mother. The conversation turned to adult relationships as they started discussing some woman's husband. They were saying things like, "Well, aren't all men the same?" and "Well you know it's the women's fault. If they did what they are supposed to at home, their husbands would behave." The mature nature of their conversation grabbed my attention, and as I listened, the things they were saying got more idiotic. As usual, my thoughts popped out of my mouth! "Not every man would do things like that!" I blurted.

My interruption made everyone look back in shock; they had forgotten I was sitting there. My mother, without thinking or saying a word, just turned around and, with the back of her hand, smacked me so hard and loud across the face that silence filled the room.

Everyone quietly returned to her tasks in an uncomfortable hush. Marcella, a Sunday school teacher from our church, hesitantly broke the stillness with, "Sister Joseph, you're really hard on that child that really wasn't necessary." That was only time I remember anyone standing up for me. Everything about me unnerved my mother. Perhaps, she wanted to protect me from the dangers she perceived my openness and outspokenness would bring "Why do you have to be different, why can't you just be like your sisters?" was always her defense.

I was one more mouth to feed, and there were times when my mother actually forgot to feed me. At dinnertime, my father came first. After that, she served plate after plate, in order of importance. By plate number ten—mine—there usually wasn't enough left. When she realized she had not fed me, she would splash water into the empty pot to loosen the scrapings from its bottom. When there was nothing left to scrape, she would pick bits of food from my siblings' plates to concoct my dinner, annoying my hungry siblings in the process.

My mother was always telling me that bad girls like me went to hell when they died. She said that hell was a place where everyone was screaming and howling from constant pain and I did not want to go there. I kept thinking, "What's the big deal about this hell place, anyway?" It sounded just like where I was already living.

All I wanted was for them to show me a little compassion. It would have been great if, by example, someone in the family would show me what being a good person was like. I was continuously being told to be good, but I didn't have a clue what that meant. They were all acting evil. All I wanted was for them to love me for who I was. After all, I was part of the family, even though I was different and difficult.

Bloody Fridays

MY FATHER CAME FROM a family of alcoholics. I learned from my siblings that our paternal grandmother did her drinking at home, while our grandfather, his three sons, and two daughters were open, falling-in-the-gutter drunks. Alcohol was in my father's blood.

I never met my grandfather; he died long before I was born. I did not really know my grandmother either, but she did come around occasionally to reprimand her son after someone was seriously hurt during one of the melees at my house. This mission took great effort on her part. She was frail and could not travel alone, so she was usually accompanied by one of her other grandchildren.

Her visits were a big deal for us on many levels. First, she cared enough to make the trip. We knew she was the only person who could talk to our father and he would sit and listen quietly. Her appearances were rare, and my oldest siblings were especially happy to see her. Perhaps they hoped that maybe, *this* time, she would say something to our father that would really touch him, possibly sink in and make a difference.

Ma Francis, as we called her, looked like a raisin with arms and legs. Her skin just hung off her as if she didn't have bones to hold her together. She was toothless, so it was funny watching her eat. She was not sloppy though. She had mastered the art of chewing with her toughened gums and when she spoke, it was almost impossible to understand. But she'd rattle earnestly, "Sonny, what you doing to yourself? What's the matter with you?" pointing to her head. "Stop this, my boy. You keep dragging your family through shame and misery. Son, people talk. You're embarrassing yourself, me, the whole family!"

My father barely said a word. He would only respond with, "Yes, Ma." or "No, Ma." He would turn into a respectful subdued infant.

"Your children, look at them, they not kids anymore. They growing up fast and will turn their backs on you. Mark my words, you will be sorry!"

She left as quickly as she came and her appearances only made things worse. My father never appreciated that she had made a trip just to scold him. He never expressed his displeasure with words in her presence though, but the tightening of his jaw and the lowering of his eyes said it all

- because even bullies respect their mothers. Maybe if she'd stuck around a little longer, he would have been tamer for longer periods, simply out of respect for his mommy.

My father usually started drinking on Friday evenings, but not exclusively. He went on drinking binges that lasted days. He made a living from whatever crops we harvested on our mother's family properties. Most of the money came from large quantities of bananas he sold to the government for export, and other crops my mother sold in Castries outside market all day on Saturdays.

To cultivate the bananas and cut down the huge trees needed to make charcoal, we would leave the house before sunrise, and walk miles to another portion of my mother's family property—snake-infested forestland to be exact. We'd try to do as much work as possible, before the punishing sun came up. We would walk the miles, barefoot, on unpaved roads through muddy trenches and toiled all day in 95-degree weather. The sweat flowed from every pore, our muddy, sticky clothes stuck to our bodies like a cheap second skin. Sunny days were bad, rainy days were worse.

Education was not a priority. We missed about two days per week of school, often accumulating to months of absences, to plow and plant the fields. Even when we tried to explain that we had tests, our father would respond sarcastically with, "Tests? What tests? Test this!" The consequence of missing so many days of school was placement in a lower level class. Fortunately, I didn't suffer that consequence and managed to scrape by.

It was also our responsibility to walk the long distances to the cash distribution center to collect the weekly payment for the banana crops. Before leaving, we had to make sure that the payment amount registered on the disbursement envelope matched the amount on the inside. Upon our return home, we handed the cash over to our father. We knew exactly how much money there was, and yet we often went hungry, lacking bare necessities.

I didn't mind being poor. What bothered me, especially as I grew older, was that we did not have to be. We certainly had a great deal more land than most people and made money from it year- round. There was no reason for us to be living in such poverty.

Every Saturday, before heading to the market to sell the crops our mother knew exactly what was expected. The night before, on Friday evenings while sober, our father would examine and value the harvest. Calculating under his breath he'd coolly murmur, "Seventy-five dollars, yes seventy-five dollars. You should make and bring me seventy-five dollars."

He'd overestimate to make sure my mother could not pocket any of the cash to give to her church.

After hours of drinking late that night, he would come home and go berserk. Slamming things, demanding, repeating the same old tired tirade, all night long, "yes...yes...yes...aha, *Pa viva sans tout lajan mwen Malpwòp fanm!*. (Don't come without all my money, nasty woman). I'm putting you on notice! Stay there all night. I don't care. Just get me my money! You think I'm stupid, but I have my eye on you. I know you steal my money and give it to that fat, lazy pastor. "Sneaky, *visiousfanm!*" (Vicious woman!) We all knew what would happen if she did not return with the right amount.

Where ever the money was coming from, our father would be waiting impatiently. He'd grab the cash, tuck it into his pants pocket and head to the three local rum shops. In one evening, he would spend every penny on vile, gagging moonshine; getting drunk and buying drinks for everyone in the shop. He was obviously capable of being generous with everyone but his family. He would roam from shop to shop until the money was all gone. Drunk out of his skull, someone would have to drag or carry him home in the wee hours of the morning. Often, his buddies would drop him off penniless on our veranda, with his pockets turned inside out.

While he was out, we were in our raggedy beds trying to fall asleep, yet tensely awaiting his arrival. Quietly, I pleaded, "If there is a God in heaven, the next knock on that door will be the police coming to inform us that he was dead." But it seemed God had turned a deaf ear on my homicidal fantasies. Not only had he turned his ear, but his presence as well. In Sunday school, we learned that all we had to do was ask, and God would answer our prayers. And so I prayed twice a day, but God did nothing. Maybe he didn't speak Creole. Whatever it was, he was just another bystander, just like everyone else.

Once home, on the days he was able to walk, our father would either stumble in the dark to the kitchen, knocking over everything in his way, or go straight to bed fully dressed in his soiled clothing. If he decided to go to the kitchen first, he would slobber through the dinner my mother had left for him hours earlier. He'd get food everywhere. Whether he was conscious enough to eat or not, my mother had to have his dinner waiting for him in his spot at the kitchen table. If the meal wasn't to his liking, which it usually wasn't, he grumbled his way through it, brewing one more reason to fight with her. "Cold. Hard. salty crap! Wouldn't feed this slop to pigs. No-good woman. Awful wife!"

Too drank to know that food sitting around for hours would naturally be cold and hard by five in the morning.

I guess he didn't realize that he was in fact, worse than a pig. With snot coming out of his nose, drool oozing out of his slobbering mouth; pants stained and reeking from peeing in his pants, filthy from being dragged through the streets. He smelled, sounded and acted like a pig. What's more, he was giving pigs a bad name!

Regardless of what he did on his arrival home, we would not get any sleep. Once in bed, he engaged in deafening, incoherent conversations—mostly with himself. These exchanges involved death rants against everyone including my mother's family, who my father despised. This detestation was mutual between him and his in-laws. He liked detailing the many ways he planned to slaughter them. *"Premye, mwen kai tiuye"* (first, I kill you) *"Alo, mwen kai tiuye tout ou fanmi"* (then, I will kill all your family).

Our father enjoyed his machete very much; he liked sharpening, cleaning, and keeping it in good working condition. A sharp machete was more than just an important farming tool to my father; he also wielded it as a symbol of his power over us, his preferred saying, *"Mwen jire kai koupe tèt ou!"* (I swear I will kill all of you).

Our mother's participation in these pillow talks was crucial. If she dozed off or didn't respond at the appropriate times with the right amount of enthusiasm at the thought of being hacked up, our father, deeming her lack of contribution a crime, would start brutally beating her.

Once the hammering began, my brothers and sisters would rush in to get him off her. At first, their intention was clearly to defend our mother. But, as this went on week after week, it became a means to vent, fight back for themselves and an opportunity to get rid of the problem. With time, this man was no longer their father, but rather an evil to eliminate.

The bloody fight would go on for hours. Even drunk, our father was a strong, formidable man, his physical strength impressive. On these nights, he was possessed even stronger than in daytime when he was sober. Like a bull in a ring, he gained momentum from the sound of the roaring crowd. One moment, he would be too unsteady and hardly able to get into bed, the next, he would be fighting off six or seven people and holding his own quite nicely.

I never understood how he did it. Our father would be standing in the middle of the angry Joseph mob, bloody, and still able to do damage to whomever he could seize. However, in the end, it was seven to one, and he was the one who would need medical attention.

One night, our father was putting up a good fight, one of my sisters, Jeanette I believe, decided that tossing him out the bedroom back door, which was about four feet above stony ground, would be the best way to get rid of him for the night. At the same time cause some serious injury. They managed to successfully dragged him to the edge of the door, but as they were about to push him out, our father grabbed on to the door frame and would not let go. They spent quite a bit of time trying to get him to release his grip by hitting, biting, pulling, and pushing him, but to no avail. They finally gave up. By that time, the cops had arrived.

Whenever a fight broke out, I had two responsibilities: remove all sharp metal objects from the kitchen, and go in search of Gilbert. Gilbert matched our father in strength and rage and I was always relieved to see him when the fighting began. My other siblings didn't stand much of a chance against our father without Gilbert's help. When my job was done, I retreated to the streets to scream my ass off—or to a corner somewhere— trying to escape to a safe place in my mind where I was peacefully asleep in a cozy, warm bed.

When I was out on the streets screaming, I know I sounded like a howling, trapped animal. My screams were a combination of high-pitched wails, which after time, when I had lost my voice, became wordless screeches. They were squeals from embarrassment, desperation, and fear that someone would die that night. An expectant crowd would have gathered in front of our house taking in the circus show. The scene never surprised them. In fact, they would have been shocked if it was a Friday night and there was no commotion at the old, crumpling Joseph residence, located at the crossroads of *Twa Chemen*, Three Roads.

The police would eventually show up but they always took their sweet time. After all, it was just another night, and the Joseph family was trying to kill its patriarch again. The police tried to keep the peace, but couldn't do much more. Often, an emergency vehicle would also accompany the officers. They would set my father on a stretcher and take him to Saint Lucia's only hospital, in Castries, to sober up, get stitches or a cast for a broken limb.

The mornings after were just as awful. The house was cloaked in a hushed, surreal cloud. We functioned like in a fog—slow, and almost robotic. The air was thick and heavy with sorrow and despair. I often hoped that this was a dream, and that I would soon awaken. But the sight and smell of human blood, combined with the potent scent of the anti-septic Dettol, served as a cold, jolting reminder that this was our reality.

It was usually up to us kids to erase the evidence left behind and try to get things back to normal. We would straighten the furniture that was tossed around, covered up or taped broken windows and other broken glass. The most heart-wrenching part was getting the blood off the walls. We may have succeeded in cleaning them, but nothing can ever wash away the indelible grief and anguish that these smells and images have evoked in my memory. I pondered the same thoughts and asked the same unanswered questions. "My family is truly messed up. Other families do not spend their weekends trying to kill each other. My God, what is wrong with us? What did we ever do to deserve this?"

There's Another Way

ELIAS' GODMOTHER, MS. JANIE, was my mother's best friend. Actually, they were more like sisters. Ms. Janie's husband, Mr. Victor, was my father's drinking partner. They lived a short walking distance from us with their only daughter Glenda, who was about the same age as Jeanette. After my mother became a born-again Christian, she tried converting everyone, including her best friend. Ms. Janie, who was happy being a Catholic, made a simple request, "If you want us to remain friends, don't try to convert or save me, I don't need saving." So my mother gave up, knowing her friend was serious. She did not want to risk losing the only friend my father allowed her to have.

Ms. Janie was a kind, yet no-non-sense person. She never watered down or repeated her words. As far as I know, she never tried telling my mother what she should do about my father. She was just always there, unwavering in her support. Initially, my mother would run to Ms. Janie's house for shelter and it was the first place my father would start searching. She soon stopped going there - not wanting to drag her friend into her mess.

My father disliked Ms. Janie, but in an odd way I think he admired her strength. He knew that she would never tolerate his ridiculous behavior if she were in my mother's shoes. In turn, he considered Mr. Victor a weakling for being respectful to his wife.

Although Ms. Janie was not my father's favorite person, he did not interfere in the women's friendship or the other couple's personal affairs. This was his way of keeping his drinking affiliation with Mr. Victor intact. I will not say that the men were good friends, since they did nothing but drink together.

Mr. Victor, even drunk himself, would make sure that my father got home in one piece. When he was intoxicated he never got out of control like my father, he was a quiet man, drunk or sober. When he went home after a night of drinking he never disturbed his family, but instead spent the night in his outdoor kitchen. Although Mr. Victor drank like my father, he was able to provide for his family and be a decent husband and father. Two things were clear -there was another kind of family out there, and my father's problem when far beyond just the liquor and his drinking, there was something seriously wrong with him, mentally.

My mother and Ms. Janie's friendship puzzled me. How could two women so different be friends? If their opposing religions and marital styles were off limits, what did they talk about?

Whatever the case, I suspect Ms. Janie was placed in my mother's life for a reason. She was an angel—the only person who was truly compassionate —never asking for anything in return. Ms. Janie gave my mother the support her own siblings and church could not give. I maintain Ms. Janie's presence and strength kept my mother going and was conducive to preserving her sanity. Ms. Janie and my mother remain best friends to this day, as are Glenda and Jeanette.

Helen of the West

NESTLED IN THE EASTERN part of the Caribbean, is the tiny island of Saint Lucia. Saint Lucia's historical background plays out like the myth of Helen of Troy. Just as Helen's beauty ignited the passions of two men obsessed with possessing her and in turn, started the Trojan War, so did the beauty of Saint Lucia ignite the passions of two countries determined to claim her. Like Helen, Saint Lucia's suitors engaged in bitter wars to possess her.

People fondly refer to Saint Lucia as "The Helen of the West." Growing up, I heard many stories as to how the island got that name. However, my favorite theory claims that Juan de Cosa, an explorer traveling with Columbus, was so smitten that he exclaimed something like, "A beauty as magnificent as Helen of Troy! My, I think we've found our Helen in the West."

Before any Europeans set foot on Saint Lucia, Arawak Indians and their enemies, the Caribs, inhabited the island. In 1499, Columbus and his crew laid eyes and boots on Saint Lucia. The British and French soon followed. By that time, both the French and British were madly in love and wanted to acquire her. Around 1660, the British colonized the island by signing a treaty with the remaining Caribs. Disputes set ablaze conflicts that persisted for over 150 years. The island would change hands fourteen times, until finally, the French surrendered and the British gained ownership in 1814.

In 1842, English became the island's official language. Although English is still the official language, local Saint Lucians speak a French Creole Patois.

In 1967, the year after my birth, England granted Saint Lucia autonomy. However, the island did not gain independence until 1979. Since then, Saint Lucia has been a stable democracy, but still operating within the British Commonwealth.

Saint Lucians elected the same prime minister from 1964 to 1996!

During Sir John Compton's tenure, the once booming banana industry was falling behind other countries; education was not improving, many students did not have the opportunity to attend high school, and there were no higher education or vocational schools to speak of. The lack of educational prospects led to young people aimlessly roaming the streets, giving rise to teen pregnancy and delinquency.

Having a Prime Minister; English as the official language; driving on the left side of the street; and a passion for cricket, are British characteristics that Saint Lucia possesses. However, the things that give Saint Lucia its flavor come from France and other parts of the Caribbean.

Saint Lucia is a mere 238 square miles in size with a population of about 165,000 people, and a great variety of vegetation and animal life. Exotic plants grow wild in the rainforests, and gardens and yards proudly display tropical flowers. The clearest and bluest of waters I have ever seen surround the island, and the sea is warm and welcoming, just like the people who reside there.

And One More Makes Eight

FOR AS LONG AS I can remember, whenever a stranger discovers that I am the youngest in my family, they excitedly exclaimed, "Oh, you're the baby! How nice. You must have been so spoiled." Part of me wishes that it were true, but another part becomes confused. Growing up, I never realized that being the last child was something special. In fact, being the youngest had always been a burden rather than a blessing.

Whenever someone commented about how wonderful it was that I was my mother's last child, my mother would always respond in a sad, "You know what they say" sort of way: *"Denye eish tuiye mama!"* (The last child kills the mother!) I could never make sense of that statement, or the reason my mother repeated it whenever someone said something nice about me, her baby.

As the last, I was the smallest and weakest; therefore, I became everyone's punching bag, picked on by a house full of angry people and lacking the strength to fight back. I was about twelve when I first heard my mother tell this story. She was at the hospital, giving birth to her sixth child in almost eight years. A nurse who had become familiar with her almost-yearly maternity visits cautioned, "Madame, you do know what you're doing to your body, right? Having all those babies so close together. Lady, you're killing yourself!"

My mother's reply was always the same, "Nurse, you think I want to be here?"

My mother repeated this story every time one of us got a year older; it seems, to remind us, especially me, of the childbearing pains she had to endure.

Birth control was not readily available in Saint Lucia at the time, and large families were commonplace. However, other women seemed better able to manage their down time between pregnancies than my mother was.

Aside from having six children who survived, my mother had given birth to two babies that did not grow past infancy. After her seventh child, Elias, was born in September 1964, this same nurse gave my mother the contact information of a woman who would give her a homemade concoction to prevent her from having more babies. She heeded the nurse's advice, taking her prescribed herbal birth control drink faithfully.

On March 9, 1966, I, Esther Joseph, was born.

Let Us Go to the House of the Lord

AS A LITTLE GIRL going to church with my mother was one of the few occasions I got to dress up and surround myself with people other than my family, so I didn't mind going.

The best thing about church though was the singing, clapping of hands, and music. My mother kept a sharp eye on me but allowed some leeway. Our Sunday school teachers encouraged us to memorize Bible verses, with prizes awarded to the person who recited them the best. I was the star of my class. Sometimes, we competed with other parishes and our church always shined. I loved competition, as it gave me an opportunity to do something I liked—speak out. It was wonderful to receive positive attention for a change. My mother made it her mission to keep me humble though. She always did or said something to diminish my accomplishments. "If only she wasn't so loud" or "She could be a little more Christian and ladylike."

Church contests were fun for a while; even so, at around ten or eleven years old, I started noticing things. Congregational members, and even those in authority, were not practicing what they preached. We read scriptures about being godlike, loving our neighbors, and that everyone was a child of God. But, if you were not part of the Pentecostal faith, you were demonized and not worthy of heaven. Saint Lucia was mainly Catholic, but Pentecostals, with their aggressive witnessing and neighborhood crusades were growing rapidly in my neighborhood. I didn't understand how people who lead honest lives and believed in God, but were not Pentecostal, would still go to hell. I started questioning the Pentecostals' very literal interpretation of the Bible.

My mother's favorite Bible verse, which Pastor Delease heavily promoted, was, "Spare the rod and spoil the child." More specifically:

"He that spareth his rod hateth his son: but he that loveth him chasteneth him betimes" (Proverbs 13:24 KJV). "Withhold not correction from the child: for if thou beatest him with the rod, he shall not die. Thou shalt beat him with the rod, and shalt deliver his soul from hell" (Proverbs 23:13-14 KJV).

This was teaching parents that children would flourish only if chastised physically or mentally for wrongdoings. My dutiful mother never spared the rod, but chastised and beat me because her God and pastor told her it was okay.

Pastor Delease however, spared the rod with his own children. His two boys and one girl were the princes and princess of the church. The more they misbehaved in church, the more doting and attention they received from the congregation. In the middle of his very long sermons, his wife and children would go have their lunch when hunger struck. The Pastor and his family lived below the church, so it was easy for them to take a break from the exceptionally long services, while the rest of us had to walk miles to get back home and have a very late lunch.

More importantly, we dare not leave halfway through the service. He would often preach a sermon about people who left early. Other times singling them out by name to embarrass them immediately. To prevent people from leaving, he eventually placed guards at the doors. He could not care less that everyone was famished, and that our stomachs were rumbling during his long drawn-out sermons.

Service ran until whenever, I guess it depended on when he got hungry. Everyone was expected to return for Sunday evening service at 6:30.p.m Christianity was hard work and Sunday was not a day of rest.

The congregation provided for the pastor taking food from their own kitchens and children's mouths—just as my mother did, showering him with their best produce.

When my father was away, my mother would send me off to the church with bags of sweet potatoes, yams and vegetables. Others provided him with, milk, meats and eggs. In doing God's work and supporting her pastor so generously, my mother frequently found herself in even more trouble at the hands of my father. He knew immediately what she was up too. The pastor taught that it was all part of being a good Christian and paving her way to heaven, so she willingly accepted her punishment in God's name.

Tithing was also part of a good Christian's duty. No matter how little they had, church members were expect to give money to the church. The pastor set monetary goals each Sunday. After the first collection, the ushers rushed downstairs to count the cash collected. If the goal was reached, he would say, "God has been good this week brothers and sisters! That means we can do better next week." He would then hike the goal amount for the following week. If disappointed, he gave a lecture about what the "church needed" and asked, "Who is holding back on God?" He would remind us,

"My dear brothers and sisters, remember that what you give to the Lord, you receive tenfold," and, "The more you give, the more you will receive."

"You can commit by verbalizing or writing your pledge on a piece of paper and placing it in the collection basket. How about you, Brother Louis? Can you be more generous with God this week?" And if he had knowledge of a brethren's windfall, a huge crop or a land sale, he was sure to bring that to the attention of the congregation. "Let's not forget brother so-and-so that God has been very good to you this week. He made that sale possible, so be as good to him as he as been to you." During these awkward moments, when people didn't come-up with the money, he'd break into spontaneous prayer. "Dear Lord, melt the hardened hearts of your people," and "Change their unwilling hearts to one of giving."

Even as a child, I knew this was insane. These people had nothing to give. They all had several kids, houses in need of repair, and barely survived. Here was an educated man, married to an educated Trinidadian, neither one of them with outside jobs, manipulating the poor and uneducated.

One of the pastor's favorite sermons was on the evils of gossiping. But in a small village community, where everyone knew each other—and each other's business, gossiping was unavoidable and a favorite pastime. Many a conversation started with, "Did you hear about so and so?" or, "Have you heard…?"

All week long, church members talked about what went on in church on Sunday. They would discuss who was a good Christian, whose testimony was most sincere and touching, who spoke in tongues or the most God-fearing, and so on. Then, their talk would turn even more superficial. They would talk about how some Sister's skirt was too short or how she was showing too much leg. Or how that other Sister was not wearing a hat, her dress was too tight or fancy, and so on.

My mother's favorite target was her rival Sister Henry. They loved to gossip about each other, and were in competition for the "Best Christian" and "Best Parent" awards. The Henry family was very different from ours. Sister Henry ruled that roost. In my mother's opinion, Sister Henry was not a good mother or Christian, since she didn't beat up her kids every chance she got.

The Henry's youngest was Tina. She was about my age and we had a like-hate relationship. Since Tina and I knew each other from church, and I wasn't allowed to hang out with non-Christians, we spent time at each other's houses. I had few friend options. Tina was therefore my friend by default. Unfortunately, Tina knew how to get me in trouble. She knew that my mother was fast and loose with the beatings, so whenever I shared any secrets with her, mean Tina would make sure it got back to my mother. I don't know how or why she did it.

One Christmas Eve, I was at Tina's house and she showed me the new shoes and dress her mother had bought her. I just absolutely had to mention that my sister Elizabeth had adjusted one of Francisca's dresses to fit me and that I too would be wearing something "new" on Christmas Day. Tina made it a point to let my mother know that I had told her about my dress. My mother took that as revealing her business and as punishment, did not allow me to wear that dress Christmas Day. Instead, I had to wear a raggedy old thing I had worn all year long. Yep, Tina taught me all about friendship and loyalty.

No matter what faults she may have had, Sister Henry always did what I wished my mother had done for me: defend her kids and never hit or humiliate them in public. My mother, on the other hand, always did the opposite to "prove" she was a better mother and Christian.

The Revolving Door

MY FATHER CONTINUED TO ravage my mother with beatings. At first, she fled to any place she knew he would not easily find her, even my father's relatives. His radar would almost immediately lead him to the home of the person that had dared to give her shelter.

Soon, my mother had overstayed her welcome everywhere, except her mother's house. While there were a few people still willing to help, my mother soon realized it was unfair to involve them and put them at risk, so she started seeking help less often.

"This is my cross, not anyone else's. God is my saver. He will deliver me," was her reply whenever someone suggested that she should go stay with a friend or relative, or run away for good.

Over the years, my mother often expressed her regret at not heeding her own mother's instinctive advice, a warning my grandmother loudly voiced early on; "He ain't right. His family not good people," she'd say disapprovingly. My mother said she carelessly disregarded her words of caution simply because she felt left out when her sisters had boyfriends and she didn't. So she accepted the invitation of the first guy who asked and convinced herself that a relationship with my father would be okay, even though she did not like him. My grandmother's disapproval of my parent's relationship started the lifelong animosity between her and my father.

At first, our grandmother attempted to help by bringing food, sometimes at my mother or sisters' request. One morning when we had nothing to eat, our grandmother dropped off a bag of small rolls. My father, coming back home saw her drop off the bread and leaving our house. Immediately he came into the kitchen, grabbed the bread, marched to the outhouse, and tossed it down the toilet. We watched in starving disbelief. He knew that if he had just thrown it in the trash, we would have taken it out and eaten it anyway. He had warned repeatedly that he did not want anything that came from our grandmother in *his* house and made it clear that disobeying him resulted in punishment.

Little by little, both my father and mother's families physically stayed away. However, my mother's family responded to my father's aggression with hostilities of their own by starting a campaign to get him off their property. They could not legally evict him, as my father married to my mother had as much right to the land as they did. Consequently, they took matters into their own hands and did everything they could to make it difficult for him to work and profit from the land. Their animals would "accidentally on purpose" find their way to and feed off our father's crops. After spending days plowing and planting, his newly planted crops would mysteriously be out of the ground. Without warning, land boundaries would change and we were told we had no right to certain areas or property that we had been allowed previously. Our father was contented to retaliate, hurting or killing the animals he found grazing on his farmland.

Caught between her siblings and husband, their actions made my mother's pathetic life even more excruciating. My father was able to stand up to them and even enjoyed playing their games. My mother on the other hand, was reluctant to deal with any of them.

Blinded by their hatred for my father, my mother's family became immune to the effects their actions were having on us. They could not separate their dislike for him from the family connection they had with my mother and her children. By extension, we bore the brunt of their vengeance. The hostilities between the families brought more conflict and ugliness into our lives. What started as retaliation against my father snowballed into a land grab by my mother's siblings, they systematically cut her off from receiving a portion of inherited land that was suppose to be divided equally between my mother and her five siblings. Soon the battle between my grandmother, aunts, uncles, and my father grew into a war between my mother's family and my immediate family. Their actions, all the feuding, gave my father more excuses to taunt and beat up my mother.

Before long, my older siblings and mother were involved in fistfights with my aunts and uncles and their families. Often, we would come home from school at mid-day for lunch, greeted by police officers who came in to break up the scuffles between them. As always, I'd miss the main event. I'd take my sweet time getting home, often passing by the fruit trees for a snack or just daydreaming in some shady field.

I remember one particular fight that my siblings reiterated to me, where my sister Elizabeth bit my uncle's sister-in-law. When I arrived, this young woman was already on her way to get stitches at the community health center.

Tell Me Why!

MY MOTHER WAS ALWAYS crying. I wondered then as I do now, why my mother stayed with my father, a man who brutalized her for years. My mother and I had a conversation once after she returned home following a particularly bad episode, one that had sent my father to the hospital for a couple days.

On the evening of her return, my mother stood at the charcoal fire pit sobbing while frying fish for dinner. Her flowing tears fell into the frying pan generating the hissing, sizzling sound that hot oil and water makes when they come together. She tried wiping away the blinding tears as she struggled to turn the fish to keep it from burning. I could not comprehend why she'd come back. Although I was only ten years old, I knew my mother had to stay away before someone was seriously hurt or killed, or just to end our misery. If ever there was a time for her to have made her grand get-away, this was it.

I sat on the long wooden kitchen bench watching my mother fry fish with her tears, when the words spontaneously popped out, "Mom, why do you come back?" I thought she was going to ignore the question, but her response was surprising.

"Where can I go?" She said slowly brimming with sadness. "I still have three children to take care of. Who will take me in with my three kids?"

At that time, Lawrence, Elias, and I were still minors (Francisca too, but she had a job and was capable of taking care of herself). This was not the only time my mother had used her kids to rationalize staying. First, she had five who could not take care of themselves, then four, and so on. I knew my mother had not wanted to have so many children. I felt responsible, if only I had never been born, I thought, maybe she would have made her escape by now.

"Why didn't you leave him the first time it happened?" I continued.

"I was eight months pregnant with Gilbert. We were having supper and the food was a little too salty, so he threw the food at me, unbuckled his belt and hit me with the belt buckle. The buckle had to be removed from my belly."

"It's been that bad, always? Why do you stay then?" I pressed, further confused.

"I was young and pregnant. What could I do? Run back home to momma? He promised it was never going to happen again. Then Joseph, and things just kept getting worse."

By that point, I realized she had forgotten about me and was just talking and justifying to herself.

"I wanted all my kids to have the same father. If I left him, what would I do? Find other men to support me and have more babies by him. I can't give you kids much, but I could give you all the same father and same last name."

That sounded so dumb it only caused greater bewilderment.

My mother had always been proud of the fact that we all looked alike, including having our family's signature gap between our front teeth.

Lost and perplexed, I wandered out of the kitchen. I could not understand why my mother would think that having so many kids with one man who tormented her was better than having kids with more than one man.

Being with only one man was merely part of the reason why my mother kept coming back. My mother was terrified of my father. In the past, whenever she left and tried staying away, my father would first beg for forgiveness and promise he would change or that he had already changed. When that tactic failed, and my mother tried being strong by staying away longer, he quickly reverted to his old ways openly terrorizing her and whoever was providing her safe haven. He would threaten death in a variety of ways, and since he was never welcomed into these homes, he would stand in the street and bellow his intimidations from outside.

"Cileeta? Cileeta! Kota ou ya? Mwen konnet ou la! (Where are you? I know you're in there!")

If she ignored him, he'd insist.

"You will never get away from me, you'll have to grow wings first; you'll have to fly if you want to leave me. Unless God in heaven gives you wings, I'll find you wherever you go and I'll kill you. You hear me. I'll chop you up in tiny little pieces," often gesturing in a chopping motion. "If you're not home by tonight…" "*Mwen kai tiuye*" and "*Mwen kai koupe tèt ou!*"

With these and other such words, he'd threaten to chop off her neck and feed her to the birds, and do the same to her mother and to anyone who got in his way.

So my mother, miserable and afraid, would return home as ordered. She accepted that God's divine intervention would be her only way out.

Good, Bad, or Just Different?

MY NEIGHBORHOOD GOT ITS daily supply of baked bread from our local baker, Iris. *Miss Iris,* as she demanded we address her, was mean and nasty, in both attitude and dress. She wore her hair wrapped in dirty, flour-dusted-covered scarves and wore the same dress for an entire week. When that dress got so grimy that even she could no longer bear it, she would turn it inside out and wear it in reverse for another week.

No matter how polite we kids were to her, she never responded in the respectable manner she demanded of us. Often, she would not even acknowledge us. Miss Iris was a hungry, angry pit-bull.

Miss Iris treated her customers as beggars. Her unpleasant conduct was legendary. The task of walking the half-mile uphill to purchase the family bread supply fell on my young, but responsible shoulders. Most kids were frightened of her and dreaded their trip to the bakery of hell, but I didn't mind. Miss Iris was tame compared to the clan I was used to at home. Furthermore, I could not get enough of Miss Iris's delicious crispy perfectly baked brown rolls and took pleasure in breathing in its enticing aroma as I made my way to her bakery. The old woman did not scare me. Sometimes, however, Iris' nastiness did manage to ruin the experience of acquiring my "manna from heaven."

When my family didn't have enough money to pay for our bread, I had to beg Miss Iris for the bread and promise to pay the next day. During those instances, she would humiliate me more than usual, saying things like, "Not gonna happen. What you people think? This ain't no charity!"

As I would start walking away disappointed, she would call out in her nastiest voice, "Where *you* going? did I tell you to leave?" I'd return to the bakery door and she'd sloppily toss the rolls, pretending to aim at the opened plastic bag. Often, the bread landed on the ground or her mud-caked wooden floor. I would gratefully brush the dirt off and put them in my bag.

Miss Iris found fault no matter what the bread order. If I ordered less bread then she expected a contemptuous, "That's all?" would follow the order. If I asked for more than my usual amount, she would say, "What do you think? You're not the only one around who needs bread! I have to think of other people you know. You can only have this much," and unceremoniously cut the order in half.

Sometimes, the bread she sold was clearly stale day-old bread. Even so, we would still stand outside her door, order our bread, and open our bags so Miss Iris could throw them in. I would always tell my mother exactly what happened at the bakery—if the bread fell, if she gave us enough bread or not, and if she made a big deal or made nasty comments about us paying her later.

One particular morning, after a few times of receiving hard and less bread than we needed, my mother sent me for more. Handing me the money she said, "If Miss Iris does not give you all the bread, tell her you'll come back tomorrow to get the rest when it's stale."

So, that's *exactly* what I did when Miss Iris refused to give me all the bread I ordered. Of course, I obeyed my mother—repeating her words exactly with lots of sass and dramatic intonation straight to Miss Iris' face. I will never forget her look of astonished disbelief. Her shock quickly turned to outrage as she started screaming at me.

"What? Who do you think you are, child? How dare you! You... you... you... Ugly! Skinny! Big mouth! You little good for nothin'! *Oh*, your parents gonna hear about this!" With her left hand on her hip and her right finger wagging in my face, she shouted, "*Ohnooo*, you're not gonna get away with talking to me like that, missy!"

While ranting and blasting me, she promptly proceeded to shut the bakery and follow me home, screaming the entire way. I ran home as fast as I could to make sure that I got there before she did. The entire neighborhood could hear her shouting as she came down the hill. I ran inside the house and quickly told my mother what had happened. She was as stunned as Miss Iris was.

"You said what?" she kept repeating, and then switched to, "I can't believe you did that! I can't believe you said *that!*"

I couldn't believe what I was hearing and every time she said that, I got more frightened and kept saying, "Well, I just said what you told me to say."

I felt so betrayed; I thought that at least this once my mother would support me because I really hadn't done anything wrong. I actually had been obedient and did what she told me to do.

"I didn't mean for you to *actually* tell her!" she said slowly shaking her head as if trying to clear the haze out of it.

"How am I supposed to know that?" I asked.

Without listening to me, she went on, "Know what your problem is? You think you're grown. I know your fresh mouth. You'd know better if you had any sense, discretion, or shame."

By then, Miss Iris was in front of our house explaining to anyone who showed the slightest interest. "Do you know what that ugly, black, skinny one with the big mouth and big lips said to me?" she screeched as my mother reluctantly made her way outside. Once again, Miss Iris detailed the incident, adding on and twisting my words, making them more insulting every time she relayed the story. My mother kept saying how sorry she was, laying all the blame at the feet of her rude, disrespectful daughter. My mother assured Miss Iris that she would take care of the matter and teach me some respect. And after Miss Iris left, that's just what she did, with punches and slaps.

I could not understand what all the fuss was about. I only said the truth and what everyone was saying behind Miss Iris's huge, jiggling behind. Ironically, the more degrading and unkind Miss Iris was, the more her popularity grew. Legend had it that she must have done some kind of black magic on the bread to keep customers coming back for more, even though baked under the most unsanitary conditions. Others had tried to duplicate her technique, but no one could bake bread like the spiteful Miss Iris. Her loaves were rolls of heavenly brown perfection. It seemed God created the magic recipe and had the devilish Miss Iris bake it and fling it at her customers.

***

A new family, the Davidson's, moved into a building a few houses away from our family home. The newcomers, husband, wife, and daughter Donna arrived from the neighboring Island of Barbados and quickly become one of us. Besides being nice folks, I believed my mother allowed me to spend time with Donna because she saw the potential of bringing the family to Christ. They immediately started attending church services regularly with us, and Donnas' parents even permitted her to attend church without them being present.

One morning, towards the end of the school year— on an important test day at school—I asked for the pencils and paper that I had requested my mother purchase for me the previous day. My mother said that she had no money for the supplies and that I should just go to school anyway. I told her that the teacher said without the pencils and paper we could not take the exam. She responded by telling me to quit bugging her and repeated that I should just go to school.

"Mom, I shouldn't go to school then—what if she won't let me take the test? It's important, I'll be embarrassed if I'm the only one sitting in class not taking it. And worst I'll have to repeat the grade!"

Fed up with my whining, she grabbed me by the arm pulled me to the front of the house and onto the street. With an impatient shove on the behind, said, "Esta, *aller la'cole!*" Go to school, but I remained under the huge avocado tree in front of our house and refused to go.

"Mom, I'm tired of being the only one in class who *never* has books and supplies! I'm tired of not being able to keep up. I am *not* going to school until I have pencil and paper!" I started stomping my feet and pulling out the braids in my hair in anger and frustration.

My mother returned to the house and I stayed under the avocado tree screaming. Half an hour later, she came, grabbed a branch from the tree, and whipped me with it. She hit me until the branch broke, and went back into the house, hoping I would be gone when she returned outside. I was still standing right where she left me. I was not going anywhere. She grabbed another branch and beat me again.

"Esta, *aller la'cole!*" she kept repeating, as she continued hitting me with the branch. This went on for hours.

I stood on the street corner, screaming at the top of my lungs, "I need pencil and paper! I need pencil and paper! I'm not going to school until I have pencil and paper! By that time, I had welts all over my bare legs and arms. Everyone, including my classmates on their way to school and their parents going to work, observed the display. The whipping hurt of course, but the real pain was the humiliation and unfairness of the situation. All I wanted was to do well in school and for that she punished me.

Mrs. Davidson, on her way to the store, stopped to console me. Between sobs, I told her my situation. With pity in her eyes, she begged, "Just go to school," adding that she understood my dilemma but I had to do what my mother said. I ignored her.

Before Mrs. Davidson returned from the store, my mother had laid one more on me. When my mother returned inside, Mrs. Davidson implored again that I obey.

It made my mother even madder that a neighbor had intervened and I was ignoring yet another adult's request to go to school. That just gave her more incentive to beat me yet again.

Mrs. Davidson would peek out of her house every few minutes to see if I was still standing on the street corner screaming. I was. After a while, she came out, paper and pencils in hand. She handed them to me and begged,

"Now, please, go to school. Okay?" "Thank you, Mrs. Davidson." I said, wiping away my tears.

By then, I'd come to the conclusion that I couldn't do anything right. No matter what I did, no matter how hard I tried, it would never be good enough for my mother. Even my best efforts were not adequate, and my "bad" amplified as the absolute worst.

I was certainly a better student than Elias and Lawrence, had more confidence, and able to handle tasks in a more responsible manner than Francisca did. But these good qualities were not appreciated or encouraged, but instead misconstrued. My family accused me of being smart-alecky, fresh, and trying to act older than my years.

It was becoming obvious that my mother's firm belief in the statement, *the last child kills the mother*, would eventually come true in some way.

My mother would get herself so worked up over everything I did, rattling her already racked nerves to such an extent, that a nervous breakdown seemed imminent. Her level of agitation and physical exertion while beating me so viciously could have easily brought on a heart attack. She seemed determined to make it come true, her constant chanting of the phrase, and intensity with which she said it, gave a strong possibility for its manifestation. Why would my mother believe or keep repeating that awful statement? What does *the last child kills the mother* mean? Could it be that generally, babies in families are spoiled into thinking that they deserve everything they want immediately without effort, setting them on a path of rebellion causing parents, especially mothers, heartbreak over having done an abysmal job raising them. My mother was doing her dandiest to make sure that she didn't fall into that trap.

Does it imply that by nature of me being born last, I would somehow be the cause of my mother's death? Was it then my fate, and no matter what I did, my mother's death would be the outcome? Since my mother really believed the stupid phrase, was she somehow even unconsciously providing me with reasons to want to kill her by treating me so badly? It made sense that when my mother learned there was actually biblical support for beating children to keep them on the straight and narrow path. She would hold fervently to her principle of not "sparing the rod." She was definitely not about to spoil that child.

Either way, I was in trouble.

Daddy Dearest

AFTER THE DEATH OF my godfather, my father became my only source of affection.

When his hair started to turn gray, I would patiently pluck them from his head. When I was done, he would empty out his pockets and give me all his change. With that money, I would buy my favorite treats: Icicles, Oh-so-strong candies, or Shirley biscuits. I was happy and relieved that someone liked me.

My father bought me my first and only doll when I was about nine years old. She was the only thing that was truly mine and not a hand-me-down. I loved the doll and nurtured her as if she was my baby. She had a small hole as a mouth and I shared my food with her. Actually, she had more meals than I did. For a whole month, I slept with and took her everywhere with me.

One morning, I awoke to a frightening sight - my doll spouting worms' right next to me.

"My dolly! My dolly!" I screamed. My mother quickly grabbed the doll and rushed outside. She unscrewed its head, shook out the worms, and rinsed her out. I thought my doll was human so when I saw her headless, being slammed against a rock, I screamed and cried even more. My mother shoved the doll back at me impatiently, and said, "Here."

She did not try to console me or explain that the doll was a toy and not a real baby. Or it would be okay because the worms were gone and not coming back. She offered not a single word of comfort to her devastated child. My siblings thought it was funny and I was being silly for crying over a skinny blonde piece of plastic. They obviously did not understand what the doll represented. They just laughed, while I cried.

My dolly was never the same. I still loved her but could not erase the image of her filled with gross wiggly worms. I lost interest in her and eventually stopped playing with her.

Another indication that my father had affection for me was that he never laid a hand on me. One afternoon though, he was sitting in his favorite spot—at the kitchen window—having a casual conversation with one of his drinking buddies, who was standing on the street. His friend inquired about his health and my father responded that he was doing well when in fact, he had been ill that entire day. It bothered me that he could not be honest and was always making up stories to explain his injuries. So, in a voice loud enough for his friend to hear, I shouted, "Liar!"

After he was done with his conversation, he turned to me, took off his straw hat, and smacked me lightly on the behind. "Don't ever talk to me like that again!"

I talked that way to everybody, and usually my father appreciated my sassiness. But this time, since I had embarrassed him, he got annoyed. His reaction took me by surprise. The light smack did not hurt my butt, but my feelings. He left the room as soon as I started hollering. I sat in the kitchen and cried for hours. Eventually, my father could not take it anymore and left the house. He returned with Icicles, a sweet, fruit, flavored frozen ice wrapped in plastic. They were my favorite treat—and on that day, they stopped my whining and fussing immediately.

On the nights when my father came home drunk, I would sometimes wait up and talk to him. For a few minutes, I could distract and took the edge off, just a bit. When my mother cooked my favorite meal, dumplings, salted beef and pigeon peas, I would make sure to stay awake. Before he could get to it and gross it up, I'd ask, "Daddy, can I have your food?"

He'd always respond with, "Yes...yes...yes...aha, your mother no feed you?"

I didn't always tell the truth. Whether I was hungry or just wanted more of the food I liked, I'd answer, "No, she forgot again."

Sometimes, he would figure out I was lying and gently scold me for being greedy. Other times, regardless of the truth, he used my *no* as another reason to harass and beat on my mother.

I was the only person able to talk him down from his psycho episodes. If I reached him before a full-blown fight developed, my tears and pleading could usually calm him. My siblings often asked me to be their buffer, using me to distract him when they knew a problem was brewing. I could soften him. I would call him by his pet name, "My Daddy Tal," which he liked, and made him smile. When my siblings needed his permission to do something or to go somewhere, they'd solicit my help to break the ice before they dare approach him.

I could not then, nor can I now, reconcile between my father's ability to show me affection, and the dark satanic side that he unleashed on the rest of the family. This was made evident one night when my sister Elizabeth, four months pregnant at the time, was working at her sewing machine in the living room, listening to a Christian station on the radio. It was a holiday weekend, Easter I believe, and she was busy trying to finish some dresses, as two customers waited in chairs next to her.

My father was in bed in the next room, annoyed by the religious sermon and my sister's enjoyment of it. Her every "Halleluiah" fired up his anger. I knew he was getting angrier with every intentional, loud clearing of his throat.

All of a sudden, he stumbled into the living room, abruptly turning off the radio. My sister immediately got up, switching it back on, returning to her sawing machine with her back to the kitchen. This continued a few more times. My father casually went to the kitchen, grabbed his machete, and strolled back into the living room. He positioned himself behind Elizabeth, and whacked her on the neck with the side of the machete blade. I will never forget the loud, high-pitched, metal-against-flesh sound of the machete hitting my sister's skin. Elizabeth shrieked in shock as my siblings and I rushed to her. My father indifferently returned to bed as the customers made a quick getaway.

When Elizabeth's daughter Grace was born months later, she had a growth on her neck that continued to develop quite rapidly. It was on the same side, our father had hit Elizabeth with his machete. That incident crystallized the full scope and consequences of our father's actions. His very first grandchild spent the greater part of her first years undergoing tests, surgery and treatments, for a cancerous tumor that he by extension, had given to her. Little Grace spent so much time in that hospital, that she learned how to walk during one of her numerous stays there. My mother, siblings and I, never our father, visited her every Sunday after church. Whenever she saw us coming, she ran happily towards us, the huge bump on her neck jiggling as she moved.

The feeling of combined love and disgust that I felt for my worm-filled dolly was equivalent to the way I felt about my father. Although I loved him, I could not overlook the wormy things that he did that infested our relationship and the entire family. But how could I not love my father? Like the doll, he filled my affection void, but I could not ignore his worms.

I loved him, yet he repulsed me. I felt guilt over the soft feelings I felt for him. I could not confess to my siblings how I felt; they all hated him, and expected me to hate him too. I convinced myself that I must be a dreadful person for loving someone who made my life and the lives of those closest to me, so unbearable. So I started to accept that the only love bad children deserve was the kind that came from bad people.

Such emotional turmoil was taxing on my young mind. I could not make sense of the baffling inconsistencies or overcome the heavy agitation I felt. Part of me knew that it was not right to accept or return his warmth, but somehow knew that without it I would not make it out of the madhouse sane. In a house filled with loonies, he was the only clown who offered any tenderness or protection so I accepted it gladly. After all, wouldn't a starving person accept contaminated food because there was nothing else available?

Had I received any degree of care from my mother, I would not have depended on my father's warmth. Like the milk from a mother's breast, a mother's love is the primary—and for a while—the main source of a child's sustenance. Craved for by every child, is that mother-child connection. It is also a required component instrumental in making sense of other types of love, including self-love. A mother's love is the mold that shapes a child's moral compass and guides them into adulthood. The quality of a parent's love is the standard by which children measure the quality of all other relationships, and as adults—an internal guiding system to assist them in differentiating between healthy and unhealthy relationships.

In those early years, I had no choice but to accept my father's affections, even though in the end, it caused me more harm than good. Later as an adult, this made me so susceptible and desperate, that I accepted any sort of gentleness and attention, especially from the opposite sex, as love.

My mother's malicious words and actions tampered with my ability to give and receive love, while my father's manipulations unraveled my mind's ability to focus and think clearly. These two sickening influences from my primary caretakers wired my psyche with a whole lot of self-hating thoughts and senseless mind chatter.

By the time I was a teenager, I had learned that emotional pain was as bad as, or often worse than, physical pain and that I needed to protect myself. The bruises from my beatings healed, and the scars would fade with time, but the ache in my heart lingered and was not dissipating. I realized that if I were to endure, I would have to be tougher, stronger, not just physically, but mentally too. So, I made a resolution. I would be in control of my feelings at all times. I vowed that in the future, I would be the one to choose how and whom I loved. Never will I be at the emotional mercy of anyone ever again.

In His Image

MY BROTHER JOSEPH BUILT a brick house on my mother's family land, next to our house. He started a business growing and cultivating ginger, and selling it to the Marketing Board, a large government operated organization that purchased food produced in bulk, and resold those items to hotels, restaurants, and supermarkets.

One day, Joseph received a huge order, which had to fill on short notice. My mother and a few of us were outside helping him dig, wash, dry, and package the ginger. My father hated my siblings, so he resented when my mother helped any of her children. Several times during the day, he called out to her to stop what she was doing. My mother's soft spot for Joseph made her strong, so she ignored her husband's orders.

As evening approached, we were still outside working. My father came out, gave my mother a lengthy, dirty look and drifted back towards the kitchen. Still standing outside, he reached in through the kitchen door and grabbed his machete, which he kept with all the other machetes under the charcoal fire pit. He also grabbed a file to sharpen his already very sharp machete. He sat in the kitchen doorway, about twelve feet away from us, cleared his throat, and then proceeded to make a big production of sharpening the cutlass. He began sharpening it slowly at first, and then building up to a faster, steadier pace. My mother, scrubbing the mud off the ginger in a large tub of water, began to tremble. She was shaking so hard that the tub started to rattle causing the water to make small rippling waves. Sitting right next to her, I felt her terror. This image I will never forget.

With the menacing sound of the machete and file metals rubbing against each other, my father fixed his gaze deliberately upon my mother, piercing fear right into her.

Elias got up from his seat and slowly walked to the kitchen, taking out his own machete and file. He too sat a short distance away, planting his stare on our father. Intentionally, he started to mimic our father's exact movements demonstrating that two could play that game. At that point, my mother's hands began to shake even more as uncontrollable tears flowed down her face, falling into the tub of muddy water.

The tension was building as my siblings stopped their work and word-lessly prepared to take our father on. Our father never attacked when he was sober though. He got angry and indicated his displeasure through glaring expressions, and repeated throat clearings, but not the physical vio-lence—not yet. Sobriety was our father's Achilles Heel, and liquor empow-ered him the way Samson's hair gave him his super human strength.

Our father cleared his throat harshly, forcefully dropped his cutlass in the pile with the others and stomped up the hill to the rum shops to fuel up. This was his way of letting us know that this was only "round one," and that he'd be back later to finish things off. While he was gone, my siblings who had been away during the day, got word of the incident and came home to wait for him and "round two." As expected, upon his arrival around four in the morning, our father began his rampage against our mother. That night was one extreme confrontation, so much so that even Joseph got involved.

Looking back, I can understand why Gilbert got involved in such destructive behaviors at night. Even though he no longer lived at home, he would usually hang around the area just waiting for the other shoe to drop. Waiting throughout the night into the wee hours of the morning until our father returned from the rum shops. Wanting to make sure, we were all right. Like a boxer sparring while waiting in the wings before the main event, Gilbert had to gear up. These late night altercations with strangers kept his anxious blood flowing.

Seeing Elias, her youngest, least aggressive son, imitate his father's hom-icidal behavior really shook our mother and awoke her to the ramifications of her decision to stay with him all these years. It finally got that the insanity had to end and she was the one who could stop it.

At last, she grasped that her children were turning into their father and that in order to protect her from him; they had to reflect their father's vil-lainous behavior. In order to take him on, they had to create themselves in his image.

My siblings were becoming impatient with the humiliating spectacle that was our family. They had started leading their own lives, and it was causing them embarrassment. I was beginning to feel shame too. By then we all just wanted the curtain to come down.

Another eye-opening incident that made my mother realize that she had no choice but to leave my father, involved Jeanette. One Saturday, Jeanette arrived home from work with a treat—a special fish we all loved. *Mashway* was expensive, rare and delicious. We were excited for that evening's dinner. While my mother seasoned the fish, Jeanette was getting ready for a night out.

A few months earlier, Jeanette had purchased the family's first electric anything—an iron. She was very proud of this modern expensive appliance.

For a long time Jeanette had been ashamed that our family was the only one in the area without electricity, so she had it installed and became the account holder. My older siblings split the bill. Our father did not contribute a penny, yet he nagged relentlessly about it. He was angry that they hooked up the electricity behind his back, after he had said we did not need it. While most of our neighbors had electricity in their homes, we were still using kerosene lamps to light up our place. The gas fumes were stinky and toxic, and highly flammable. Our house was a fire just waiting to happen.

Every discussion and attempt at getting him to improve the place always ended the same way, "This is my nest! You ungrateful good for nothin' bastards! Don't like it, get your own. You kids think you're so fancy, fancy! Today, it's electricity. Tomorrow, fridge, stove. Go put your frickin' fancy some place else!"

My father was right about one thing. Our house was a nest all right, but not one that birds would want compared with their nests.

Our father was always accusing Jeanette of showing off and pushing the rest of us into wanting things, calling her uppity every chance he got.

That Saturday, Jeanette was ironing an outfit she was planning to wear that night. My father incensed that she had brought home the special meal, causing everyone to be in a good mood anticipating having a nice dinner for a change. He started complaining again that the iron was using too much electricity. Pushing back his chair so wildly that it tipped over, he marched over to the table where she was ironing and unplugged the iron. My sister re-plugged it and said, "You're not paying for it, so don't worry about it."

He unplugged the hot iron again, grabbing it from her and lifting it to her face he barked, "How about I plug it up your ass?!"

Jeanette gathered her garments and retreated to the safety of the bedroom.

In an effort to upset Jeanette further, he tramped back to the kitchen, grabbed hold of the pot with the fish from the charcoal stove, and tossed it out the kitchen door onto the dirt outside. Those of us in the kitchen, hungrily waiting dinner were stunned, but not surprised. It was just another day our father was willing to let us go without a meal. My mother, helpless as always, said nothing.

Our father's behavior affected Francisca the most that day. She rushed out to try to salvage some of the dinner and her favorite fish. She was down on hands and knees weeping, trying frantically to dust the dirt stuck onto the fish. My mother grabbed the soiled fish from her, repeating softly, "Stop, don't eat that." Lawrence, Elias, and I aimlessly scattered in different directions out in the fields to get away and find fruits and other things to eat. Jeanette quietly got ready for her date.

Out of all of us, Jeanette hated our father the most, and the feeling was mutual. Janette traveled in a more educated circle than the rest of my siblings, so she was the most embarrassed by our circumstances. We lived in a tiny five-room wooden house steps from the main road—a three-way-junction. My father had intentionally allowed our house to deteriorate, over the years. The paint had completely peeled off the rotting wood, the galvanized sheets that once were the roof, were so old and rusty they could no longer be held down by nails, causing the roof to leak and flap uncontrollably in the wind. My brothers periodically climbed on the roof to lay bricks on the sheets, to prevent them from blowing away. The entire house had holes so big in the flooring that we could see the outside dirt under the house while standing inside. The small veranda also had holes in its floor, and the wooden designs that once connected it to the rest of the house were no longer intact, causing the balcony to separate from the rest of the house and cave in. Discomforted by our house, we rarely invited friends over to visit.

My father refused to fix the house as some sick form of punishment and thrive on our uneasy. My older siblings would have loved to combine their resources and patch up the old house, but were reluctant to spend money on a house that was unpleasant to live in, and that our father would not appreciate, take care of, or allow us to enjoy. Fresh paint, a new roof, new furniture, or new floors would not transform any house, especially our rotten one, into anything resembling love and respect.

Sure, I would have liked to live in a pretty house, but it wasn't the decrepit old house that upset me the most, but the repulsive behavior of everyone in it.

We all thought that the alcohol and our father's careless, violent lifestyle would contribute to his early death, ending our troubles. The older we got, the more we realized he was not slowing down and might outlive us. Jeanette was the most outspoken about ending our shame. She was convinced that we needed to take matters into our own hands, and that the only solution was to murder our father, permanently doing away with the source of all our problems. She was seriously considering creative plots to kill him without being caught. Poisoning him was the easiest. Another plan involved setting a venomous creature on him while he was working alone in the woods, this one was risky and the least favorable.

The last plot she concocted was a darn good one. It involved tampering with the house's faulty electrical wiring, setting the house ablaze while he was in bed passed out drunk. This was the most feasible since many houses were going up in flames due to bad wiring and poor electrical system on the island. It was not farfetched that our father would get barbequed in his blazing nest.

We hated our father, but could we really carry out these plots and bear the burden of his homicide on our conscience?

Out of the Frying Pan, Into the Fire

I WAS ALMOST FOURTEEN years old when my mother finally left my father. For good!

My Aunt Theresa, who lived in the United States, provided money to build a brand new house for her mother, my grandmother. The new house was steps away from her old home. Fortunately, out of pity for my mother, and guilt over my mother's stolen inheritance, when her new house was completed, my grandmother gave my mother her unwanted one. This offer prompted my mother to do what she should have done years prior.

After one of my parents' clashes, while my father was in the hospital being stitched-up, my mother knew it was time. Now that she had a place of her own, she had no more excuses. Without much ceremony, my mother packed a few personal items, her four youngest children and left.

My mother, Francisca, Lawrence, Elias, and I moved into our grand-mother's unpainted one bedroom log shack a few miles away from our old family home, where my father now lived by himself. The only improvement to our new living situation was our father's absence.

I hated living so close to my grandmother, *Mom Ta*. I barely knew her; she was emotionless, gossipy, and nosey. My grandmother's nosiness knew no bounds! It was so outrageous and obsessive, that it was creepy and earned her the unflattering title of *gajay*, (witch). It was beyond uncomfort-able living so close to her, and we were teased by children and adults. "Your grandmother's a witch! She's a devil and flies on a broomstick at night!" they'd say, pointing at us when walking by us on the streets, or our house.

Unfortunately, her appearance gave credence to her title. She was extremely bowlegged, and wobbled when she walked. She made use of a walking stick to get around and always had her hair wrapped in a scarf. She was wrinkly, very tall—about five foot nine inches—and skinny.

My grandmother was accused of witchcraft because she knew details about neighbors and even the intimate lives of strangers. When my grand-mother saw two people having a conversation, she went to great lengths to find out what they were discussing. She would use anything that offered cover; hiding behind buildings, poles, and when in a store, shelves. Her favorite, most convenient and least conspicuous spying spot was her own garden, situated right on the edge of her street. Crouched between plants and shrubs, she would get an earful of unsuspecting passersby's conversations. My tactless grandmother just could not keep the secrets she overheard. She took pleasure in later approaching the parties involved, to let them know that she knew their secrets. She would not blackmail anyone with the information, but rather, reveal in a concerned manner or ask questions to get more details as though they had directly confided in her. She would say things like, "Did your husband *really* sleep with your niece? Oh, you poor thing. You're being so brave through it. You could do much better anyway." Or, "I heard you left your cheating husband. Good for you, honey. It's about time!"

In addition, if she heard people gossiping about someone else, she'd go to them and tell them that their so-called friends were saying "this and that" about them.

Puzzled as to how she knew these personal things about them, the community decided she had to be a witch. After these encounters, upon recovering from their shock, people often hurried away in disbelief shouting, "*Gajay, gajay ale!* (Witch, Witch go away!) How do you know my business?"

People came to her home to toss holy water at her. They would accuse her of casting spells on them, blaming her for everything wrong in their life. Some folks, who had consulted white magic witches, would throw other items or concoctions, in an attempt to reverse her spells. They would cause a scene as we looked on incredulously. The move to my grandmother's house had not made much of a difference to me. We had just moved from one disgrace to another.

Since my grandmother and father hated each other, he too accused her of casting spells on him. My father always used that against my mother and never wanted *his* children "to have any thing to do with that witch." He blamed his evil mother-in-law for *all* his misfortunes.

It took years before a few of my grandmother's neighbors decided to turn the tables and spied on her. They figured out she was just a bizarre snoop, but by then the hideous title had stuck, and she remained known as a witch until the night she died peacefully in her sleep.

Living in such close proximity to her, and seeing what was going on, worried me. I could not help but wonder if she had indeed put a curse on our family. I kept my distance just in case.

Francisca had a job at a family supermarket in the city. She stayed with the family during the week and came home on weekends. My mother and Francisca got along smashingly. They shared their fervent religious beliefs and church activities, while I hated and refused to go to church. Although I acted like, and tried convincing myself that their bond did not bother me, I envied and was deeply hurt by it. The feeling that I was an outsider looking in on a loving mother-daughter relationship hurt the most. Left out, I felt more alone than when I was surrounded by more siblings and my father. How could a mother treat two daughters so differently?

I suppose since Francisca made an effort at being a good daughter, my mother could easily show her affection. I, on the other hand, had given up all effort in trying to satisfy her. I was not deliberately being difficult or giving her a hard time however, by that point, I realized no matter what I did it was never going to make her love me.

At this point, Lawrence and Elias were teenage boys and allowed to roam freely, late into the night, while I not permitted to go anywhere unsupervised. When I pointed out the unfairness of that policy, my mother's reply was always the same: "Boys don't get pregnant and bring babies home." Being away from my father had a positive effect on my brothers; not having to engage in battles with him mellowed them out a bit. Although they had not become loving brothers to each other or me, they were starting to enjoy their life.

I was still attending high school and was at home more often than my bothers and sister. As my mother's sole responsibility, I now became the focus of her not-so-loving attention. By this time, she deemed me extremely out of control, liking all the things her church did not approve of, she needed to reign me in before it was too late. With time on her side and no distractions, she was going to straighten me right up!

For thirty years or so, my mother lived everyday in fear. During that time, her thoughts had been just an extension of my father's. Basing every decision on what would save her skin. She could not have known who she was as her own person. Now, with that fear behind her, she was facing new ones. Like an ex-con, she did not know how to live in freedom, or how to deal with the resentment she was carrying. My mother could not exist without drama, so subconsciously she had to find new ways to create more of it, so she turned my small misdemeanors into huge productions.

My one wish was for my mother—instead of grabbing on to a whip or belt after I had done something she considered unacceptable—latched on to me and say, "Esther, you are my daughter, there is nothing you can ever do that will make me stop loving you." That would have ended all my misdeeds. I would have done anything to make my mother happy.

As a teenager, my mother would force me to go to church and for a while, I went realizing that not resisting made my life easier. Just the same, I could no longer ignore the uneasiness that the Pentecostal's narrow interpretation of the Bible gave me, along with the hypocrisy of the church members. I was no longer interested in playing that game, so I stopped going.

I got into trouble for questioning the church's teachings and double standards the church members lived by, especially the pastor. My mother was not having any of it, demanding that I go to church. I refused. She would come home after her church service and beat the crap out of me. This became our Sunday ritual. My mother was determined to continue my father's tradition of disrespecting the holy day.

I imagine her—sitting in church—her anger building, fuming, plotting her attack during the hours-long service, the same way my father did sitting at the kitchen window planning his revenge on her for attending church.

She would attack as soon as she walked through the door. I was fine with the beatings, I had become desensitized, and they no longer afflicted me. I refused to give her the satisfaction of seeing me cry. No matter what she did or what she used to hit me with, I showed no emotion. Soon, even the welts and bruises she left on my body no longer disturbed me. I stood in defiance proving to her that she could no longer hurt me. My immunity to her cruelty enraged her even more, and the beatings would get more severe as she tried penetrating my emotional armor.

One Sunday afternoon, when my mother had used up the tree branches and other things she had available to beat me with, she started punching and slapping me. She was hitting me with all her might. With eyes bulging, foaming at the mouth, on the verge of exploding, she kept repeating, "*Denye eish tuiye mama!Denye eish tuiye mama!*"

I thought for sure she was going to have a stroke or heart attack. And indeed, it seemed like I would be the death of her. When her arms got tired, she grabbed my arm and bit me. When I did not react, she reached for a piece of a rubber watering hose on the ground next to us and started hitting me with it. That hurt!

My mother tried breaking me. I knew that was her goal, but I would not give her the satisfaction. When it came to saving my soul, my mother was not a quitter. After a while, I would stand with a defiant smirk during the beatings, to let her know that her energy was wasted. Of course, that maddened her even more. By now, I too was convinced that the Saint Lucians and my mother's saying would come to pass. One way or another, I—her youngest child—was going to kill her.

My mother thought that I would soon get myself in all sorts of difficulties, mainly getting knocked-up and bringing babies home for her to take care of. I was different from all my sisters, but Francisca and I were total opposites, and that freaked my mother out. She assumed that my sister's time at the church made her immune to getting pregnant, while I was doomed to hell for not believing in God and going to church. I was immoral, evil, and a *jammet*. My love of dance, make-up, and jewelry meant I was a no-good slut whose soul needed saving.

Previously, as an unquestioning child, I believed I deserved punishment for being bad, and accepted my siblings' beatings when I did something that angered them. After all, I did use their personal items even when they specifically asked me not to. I felt that I was a burden to my mother too, when I was disobedient and made her life more demanding. I should not have been adding to the unpleasantness of her life. I felt bad for her and thought her anger was justified.

However, I grew to learn the difference between punishment for valid offenses and punishment just for being myself. My mother tormented me for everything, all the time. She beat me for doing, or not doing something, saying too much or not saying enough. During these whippings, she would beg me to stop being bad so she would not have to beat me. It was becoming clear that being hit by your mother just for being in her presence was not normal. I saw how my friends were treated by their families. My behavior was often better than theirs was, yet I received more severe penalties.

As a child, we had a battery-operated radio. Whoever bought the batteries had first dibs on what stations played for that week. I had no chance. Since we had no electricity, that one radio was our only source of entertainment. Often, if my mother or sisters got to it first, it would be a Christian station playing.

When I was older, we upgraded to a little boom box and we could play cassettes. By then, my exposure to music was greater, and while reggae and calypso were the popular music in Saint Lucia at that time, pop music was what stole my heart and got me into trouble.

My friend Christina was a member of our high school dance group, and I hung around after school to watch them practice their routines. This was as close as I could get to actually dancing, since my mother did not allow me to join the dance group. My classmates had more exposure to culture and other activities that I could only wish to get involved in, like beauty pageants, and dancing in Saint Lucia's Carnival festivities. They were dancing to different kinds of music and knew about musical artists I had never heard of. Christina was the one who made my first mixed tape, which had four ABBA songs on it, including my favorite song, *Dancing Queen*. I fell in love with ABBA's music and could not stop playing and dancing to it.

I could not help myself! Even in church I would get carried away when the congregation would sing, clap, and stomp their feet. The tambourines and various small percussion instruments turned me into a dancing queen right there, in church! Naturally, that always got me into more hot water. Decorum was the rule in our religion, but dancing and music were my drugs—I was addicted, and could not control myself.

As far as my mother was concerned, I was either dancing too hard, singing too loud, and having too much or not enough fun. If I arrived at church after she did, wearing make-up, she would come to wherever I was sitting and harshly try to rub off the make-up with her hands, smearing the colors all over my face, deliberately making me look like a clown. She loved embarrassing me in public.

A not- to- be -forgotten church beating occurred one day when a sister testified. The pastor had started encouraging the congregation to practice speaking English. That day, the sister testified in English, or at least that is what it should have been. Her testimony was a jumbling of Patois and broken English. It was as if the Spirit possessed her and she was speaking in tongues. One of the few words we could understand was *ginger*, which was a big money-maker on the island at the time. Everybody knew about her conflicts with her neighbor over a ginger plot. In relating her story, she created a language all her own. I could not contain myself. No matter how hard I tried, I could not stop the giggles. Francisca giggled too, but was able to control herself, as usual. Everyone was staring at me. Francisca and I were sitting a few pews behind my mother, and she kept shooting nasty looks my way. Even after the sister had passionately spilled her heart out, my giggling continued. Perhaps they were becoming giggles of nervousness since I knew what was coming. I earnestly tried to stop laughing.

My mother left her seat and came to my pew. Others looked on in silent approval as she drummed on me. Perhaps my embarrassment and the nerves that built up from not being able to control myself made me more vulnerable to my mother's actions.

I never cried during these church beatings because I was always so humiliated, and wanted to prove to her that she was not capable of getting to me. But this time, she did. Tears of laughter soon turned into tears of shame and degradation.

The Day My Music Stopped

IT WAS EXCRUCIATING GROWING up in a house where listening to non-religious music was forbidden. My two older bothers, Lawrence and Elias, were not subject to this or any other regulations, doing as they please. No matter how hard I tried, and Lord did I try, I couldn't stop myself. Without noticing, I found myself twirling, boogying, and in trouble yet again.

No matter where we were, my mother would go ballistic, "God help me!" was often her first plea. Then the screaming and beating would begin, "Why would you want Satan to use you that way? Shaking her head, "May God have mercy on your soul!"

Somehow, the whippings always ended with almost the same questions: "Why do you want to go to hell?" or, "Are you that possessed that you like being hit?" Walking away, she would mumble to herself, "*Denye eish tuiye mama*," reminding me that I am supposed to kill her and for that, I would unquestionably go to hell!

Of course, I did not want to burn. Still, during those degrading moments, hell was never my concern. I just wanted her to stop hitting me. On top of the welts and bruises, most of my hurt came from knowing that her double standards applied to only me.

One Saturday night, my brother Elias celebrated his birthday by having a huge party at our house. After much begging, my mother unwillingly allowed me to attend. She only consented because she was going to stick around to supervise.

All of Elias's friends and the neighborhood kids came out. He had tons of beer and other alcoholic beverages and one of his friends tended bar. He rented a huge boom box with giant speakers and a turntable, and another one of his buddies DJ'd. Everyone was having a great time, including me! The reggae, soca, and disco music were going strong and I was grooving.

Although my mother was allowing me to dance, I could tell by her body language and sharp darting stares that she was fuming with displeasure. I was happily dancing my way to hell!

After hours of fast-paced dancing, a slow dance finally came on. Trevor, a next-door neighbor, asked me to dance. I gladly accepted. In that moment, just as always when I am dancing and at one with music and movements, I changed. I became a person who forgets everything but the rhythm and beat, temporarily leaving this world and its troubles behind. Unfortunately, I also forgot that my mother was watching my every move.

When the music stopped and the dance was over, I slowly returned to earth and opened my eyes. It was then I realized that the others had stopped dancing to admire Trevor and me. We had an audience. Some folks whistled, some hooted, others applauded with approval. I had little time to enjoy the attention, for my eyes were instantly drawn to my mother standing in the background, her arms crossed over her chest and head tilted slightly to one side. She had that look; one I knew too well. What followed that look was always the same–punishment and indignity. That night was no exception.

In the presence of the entire crowd and without uttering a word, she came out onto the veranda where I was standing, grabbed me by the hair, dragged me through the kitchen, and shoved me into the nearest bedroom, slamming the door shut.

And so, that was the end of what could have been an awesome neighborhood party. Again, my mother was following in my father's old, worn out footsteps and becoming the death of parties. Yet that could not stop me.

Home alone one day, I inserted my recently acquired, bootlegged copy of ABBA cassette into the tape recorder and turned up the volume. I shut my eyes tightly as I began swaying to the music. I sang along in my off-key fashion, but thought I sounded just like the Swedish foursome did: *You can dance; you can jive, having the time of your life. Oh! See that girl; watch that scene, diggin' the dancing queen.*

"This can't be wrong," I kept thinking as I swayed my hips seductively. I was free, alive! These forbidden moments were all that mattered. I was safe in a universe all my own where no one could hurt me. I was the dancing queen! *Feel the beat from the tambourine. Oh, yeah. You can dance; you can jive, having the time of your life. Ooh, see that girl; watch that scene, diggin' the dancing queen.*

Before ABBA could sing the last *ah... ah... ah..., ah, ah, ah, ah, ooh,ooh,* my music stopped. I opened my eyes and saw her. Standing in the doorway of my grandmother's tiny living room, arms crossed over her chest—the mid-afternoon sunlight streaming through the open window, striking her face at a disfiguring angle reminding me of a zombie in one of my many nightmares. Standing there as big as the whooping I was surely about to receive—was my mother. If only she had known, her look was all the punishment I needed, more hurtful than a thousand lashes.

On that June afternoon I finally broke. For the first time, I promised and meant it. I would never dance again. And I kept my word, until...

Run, Esther, Run!

WEARING MAKEUP MADE ME feel beautiful. It also gave my mother one more reason to discipline me. One sunny afternoon after having a relaxing bath, I got dressed in a clean summer dress and braided my hair. Using charcoal, I arched and darkened my eyebrows. I crushed some red hibiscus petals and rubbed them unto my lips as lipstick and cheeks as rouge. I looked super pretty.

I stepped out the bedroom and was about to head out to enjoy a lovely stroll. My mother, standing at the kitchen table preparing vegetables for dinner with a sharp butcher knife, took one look at me and screamed "Jezebel!" and charged at me, the knife still in her hand. I bolted out the kitchen door, ran to the back of the house with my mother at my heels screaming, "You better not let me catch you! Come here, You Jezebel! I'm gonna chop your face right off!"

I knew that if she caught up to me, she would indeed cut me up. I just knew she would do it. What scared me more was she was using my father's infamous words, and still had the knife in her hand. I ran as fast as I could around the house a few times screaming "Mom, no stop!" She continued chasing me, screaming, "*Jammet*, you like all these nasty things! Jezebel, Jezebel!"

Joseph's wife, Agnes, came out onto her veranda to investigate. I will never forget the sight of Agnes doubled over in uncontrollable laughter, pointing at my mother, still holding the huge knife and chasing me around our gorgeous new house. We were both screaming at the top of our lungs. My mother hated makeup, and would have grown wings in order to catch her devilish daughter and cut Satan out of her face. When I realized she was not losing steam, I ran even faster in another direction towards the street. Eventually she gave up.

Whenever I did something wrong my mother never let it go, each time adding more details and one of my previous offences for good measure. She loved making predictions regarding my abysmal future, "I tell you that girl is useless. She'll never get a man. No respectable man would ever want her!"

***

When I arrived home from school, I would remove my uniform bottom —my black pleated skirt—and walk around the house in my green shirt-jacket and panties. One afternoon, I was wandering around in my under-pants, when my mother suddenly dashed from the kitchen to the living room. Grabbing me by the arm and gesturing pointedly downwards with her eyes, she hissed, "You're not a child anymore. Cover up!"

Taken aback, I looked down to where she was looking. Then I under-stood the look of alarm on her face. I started screaming hysterically, "Am I dying?" Not waiting for an answer, I started yelling, "I'm going to die! I'm going to die!"

My mother realizing that I was oblivious to what was happening asked, "You don't know?"

"Know what?" I asked nervously. All I wanted to know was whether I was dying or not.

My mother awkwardly and angrily explained, "From this day, if you let boys touch you, you *will* get a baby. And *if* you ever have a baby, I will kick you out of this house! I ain't gonna take care of your babies understand!"

"Babies? Just tell me, am I going to die!"

I felt, that I had done something horribly wrong and deserved her harsh words. Technically, I wasn't a child anymore, but I certainly wasn't a woman; I was even more confused, and of course, I believed her words.

I can recall a day in primary school, a few months before I became a "woman." Two of my classmates, Faith and Paulina, were sitting behind me in class having a hushed conversation. They were murmuring something about someone having a period. I turned around and asked innocently, "She got an extra class period to do what?"

Giving me strange looks, they started to giggle, like cohorts with classi-fied information they we not about to divulge. Before I could press them, the teacher came to the back of the class to break up our discussion.

I had three older sisters and yet, none of them had taken the time to explain the developmental changes that a female body must go through, and the things a young girl needs to know. I had no idea what to expect until the change was actually happening. I was ill- prepared and in the end, only had fear instilled in me by my mother.

For a long time, I believed and heeded my mother's caution, altering my relationship with boys in the process. I feared yet admired them. Even today in my forties, the thought of having a child fills me with trepidation.

Having my mother tell me about "babies," at a moment when I thought I was dying from bleeding from my private area, had inconceivable consequences. She instilled the idea that becoming a mother, having an intimate relationship with men, and my menstrual cycle, were all obscene things that should make me feel ashamed. Picture my surprise when I discovered that in some cultures, a girl's coming-of-age is a time of great celebration.

***

One specific beating from my mother was instrumental in shaping the woman I would later become. One of my best friend's in high school was Margarita, who was about one year older than I was. Margarita was pretty with light skin and soft, long curly hair and she was shorter me. We attended Home Economics class together and practiced our cooking projects mostly at my house. We baked cakes and made tablet (coconut drops).

We spent a lot of time together. However, not enough for me to know that she had a boyfriend with whom she was spending "quality" time. The boy's family and Margarita's had been feuding like the Montague's and Capulet's for years. The star-crossed lovers were having sex behind everybody's back, and I was Margarita's scapegoat. She frequently told her mother that she was studying at my house after school.

Our brothers were also friends. One afternoon, her brother came over to visit and informed us that since Margarita was pregnant, his parents had kicked her out of the house. He told us very matter-of-factly, assuming that since Margarita and I were "best" friends, I already knew about her pregnancy. The news took us all by surprise. I was really, truly shocked, but to my mother, I was just acting. She believed I was a conspirator and that I too was engaging in sexual activity.

The truth is that I knew very little about sex to begin with, and had not developed a sexual interest in boys. I was naïve when it came to such matters. If I had not been so clueless, I might have caught on to Margarita's scheming ways. My mother however, didn't see me that way and didn't believe a word of my denial. She clobbered the crap out of me and called me a "vicious, sneaky, deceitful slut." She really thought that I was having sex, and that I was pregnant too, or soon would be.

The complexity of human relations had always been too much for my messed-up, scrambled brain to handle. The crazy relationships I was witnessing—especially my parents were not anything close to what I envisioned for myself, so I guess I didn't give it much thought. Not wanting to end up trapped and miserable like my mother, or the women I knew. They were all, in one way or another, slaves to their men.

That afternoon, I was utterly innocent of *everything* my mother accused me of, but, in her eyes, I was *always* guilty. On that day, my faith in women, friendship and relationships of all kinds, ended. On that day, something inside me died.

***

One Wednesday night, some of the neighborhood teenagers—including myself, and cousins who lived across the street from us—gathered under the neighborhood's only street electrical light post, which was in front of my house. My mother was at one of her weekly activities at the church.

Dave, a boy who had recently become one of Elias' motorcycle acquaintances, was among the teenagers hanging around. I was fifteen and he must have been seventeen or eighteen years old. We were a little apart from the other kids having our own conversation, just chatting about nothing in particular.

I imagine that someone on their way to church must have seen me and mentioned it to my mother. It was enough for her to leave church immediately.

I saw a shadow rushing down the road towards us but didn't think much of it.

I only realized who it was when she started hitting me all over with a large branch in front of everyone. She even deliberately whacked Dave a couple of times, all in brutal silence.

In the moment my mother was hitting me, I first felt shock, then shame. My third thought was to run! I ran behind the house and sat in the dark, trying to compose myself. I tried to make sense of what just happened. I could not believe it. My mother had just given me a beating in the presence of someone I was having an innocent conversation with, for no reason! It was in that moment, I realized that what my mother just did to me, and her actions over the years, were pure insane hatred. My anger, like a slow pressure cooker, percolated. For the first time, I finally allowed myself, with great reluctance, the right to feel hatred for my mother.

***

It had taken me a long time to accept that my mother hated me or that a child in turn, had the right to hate her mother, breaking a sacred bond.

Until that night when I received a beating for innocently talking to a guy, I had justified almost everything. I was always doing something improper, being disobedient and deserving of her punishment. According to my mother—and I had bought into her rationale—it was my evilness that made her chase, beat and ridicule me. That night, while sitting in the darkness overcome with shame, and disgusted at the acceptance of this truth, it became apparent that no matter what my actions, they did not merit such degradation. No child should have to suffer at the hands of her own mother.

For several days after that unpleasant incident, I wrestled with my feelings and scores of unanswered questions. The years of painful memories flooded me, gnawing at my insides. Are these hateful emotions who I am? If it is, how could I live with myself? I can't live like this yet I have no way out! "The last child kills the mother" Isn't that what she believes and expects of me? Perhaps my only recourse is to fulfill her prophesy.

A Certain Kind of Calm

THE NIGHT HURRICANE DOROTHY hit in late September 1977, the force of its winds flattened our old family house, where my father still lived alone. Surprisingly, my grandmother's shack, where we lived, survived. We watched in terror as our neighbors' homes just flew away. Neighbors sought shelter with us from the relentless wind and rain. We were scared out of our minds; some people were reciting the "Hail Mary," while others were singing "Kum Ba Ya." They were caring and kind to each other, and acting like this was it, trying to redeem themselves before meeting their maker. Luckily, none of us were hurt or killed that night.

In the aftermath, families who did not have home insurance or could not afford to rebuild their homes, received assistance. When the government came out to survey the damage in order to determine the level of aid my father would qualify for, they ascertained that he had no legal right to rebuild on my mother's land without her consent.

Finally, it seemed like the divine intervention my mother had been praying for was manifesting. Perhaps God had been waiting for my mother to take the first step—move out, do something. After all, God helps those who help themselves. Everything fell into place after that. My mother took a stand and had my father kicked off her land. She did not have to do anything herself; the government took care of everything for her.

Government aid, support from foreign churches, humanitarian organizations, and money from my siblings, enabled us to build a brand-spanking new house on the spot where the old Joseph house once stood. We quickly moved from my grandmother's house to our new home. My father, with no money but only a hint of sympathy from my mother, relocated to another section of my mother's property. He could only manage to build a shack across the street from us with the remnants of our old house.

Our new house was the most beautiful ever. To me, it was a mansion! It had three bedrooms with twin beds and dressers, a dining room, a living room, and a kitchen with electrical appliances. At last, we had indoor plumbing with running water and an indoor bathroom. We were finally living like everyone else. Additionally, because my mother had ultimately gained independence from my father, people saw her in a new light.

However, an impressive new house and freedom did not change my mother's attitude towards me. The anger she bestowed on me in our previous houses transferred seamlessly to this new one. I was so miserable that not even a new house could make up for the lack of love and compassion I yearned for.

I even missed my father.

America Has Shed Her Grace on Us

THERESA, MY MOTHER'S YOUNGEST sister, was around nineteen years old when she left Saint Lucia for the United States. As a child, I heard the story of how Aunty Theresa had became the babysitter to the kids of an American family stationed in Saint Lucia. The family really liked her, so they asked her to come with them when they had to return to the States.

The family sponsored her, and after years of living in America, she became a citizen. Kept abreast and updated of my mother's situation through rumors, Theresa was aware of the ongoing feud between her siblings and my father over the family land, but remained impartial when her brothers and sisters ventured to include her in their land injunctions, and other legal proceedings in their battles against my father.

I met Aunty Theresa a few times on her visits back to the island. She would stop by our house for quick visits, but never stayed overnight, the way she did with other relatives. She always brought gifts, shoes, bags and clothes meant for all her relatives. But, the families she stayed with got to pick out all the best and nicest items, while my family always received the tacky leftovers.

Theresa must have taken pity on my poor mother, because in the grandest gesture, decided to sponsor my mother and set into motion the long, complicated process of obtaining permanent visas. This would allow my mother and her minor children at the time—Lawrence, Elias, and I—to immigrate to America. This procedure started while my parents were still together, as an effort to get my mother away from my father. Since my father always told my mother that she would have to grow wings in order for her to get away from him, "flying" on an airplane to another country seemed a suitable escape from his clutches. Several years had passed, and we had forgotten about the applications. And by this time, my mother had already left my father, so coming to America wasn't a priority.

Finally, when I was sixteen, Immigration approved us for entry into the United States. My mother and Lawrence left for America, leaving Elias and I behind for another year, while they settled and found work in New York. They moved in with my aunty in her one-bedroom apartment on Church Avenue in Flatbush, Brooklyn.

During that year, Elias and I remained with Francisca, Jeanette, and Neromas, Jeanette's son, in our family home. My siblings had their own lives and had no time or inclination of keeping close tabs on me, as my mother did. That gave me some breathing space and a chance to grow finally into myself. I was not leading an exciting life by any means, but I had a little freedom. I didn't start doing anything crazy, but having the burden of my mother's condemnation lifted from me was like a small plant having a huge rock lifted from it, and at last receiving the sunshine it needs. I blossomed!

Surprisingly, after my mother's departure, I returned to the Pentecostal Church on my own. Acceptance into the church's inner circle eluded me because to them, I was not appropriately chaste or demure enough to be a good Christian.

I loved fashion and makeup, and chose not to give them up. My "fashion statements" labeled me "playing Christian" but I believed that the intention in my heart determined my love for God and it didn't matter what I wore on the outside. I still resisted the craziness and fundamentalism of their beliefs, but I had always enjoyed the worship and reading of God's Word. I knew nurturing one's personal relationship with God was the basis of going to church, so I ignored what people thought or said about me. Perhaps not being forced to go to church and act a certain way, gave me the choice and freedom to seek the answers to my countless questions.

My last year in Saint Lucia was an equally confusing time for me. Although I was attending church regularly, so much was still missing in my life that religion was not filling. In my searching, I was starting to gain some perceptive. The older I got, the more I was realizing that my father's selective, manipulative type of love might have served me as a child, but won't as a growing person. In fact, both my parents' relationships with me had turned me into an emotional cripple. I was not close to anyone and did not have many friends. If one of the few I had got mad at me or vice versa, I had no problem just dropping them. I did not have the desire or patience to settle disagreements amicably. I recognized this was a problem, but I had no clue how to fix it.

Gilbert lived all over the place. He was a roamer who had inherited our father's violent treatment of women. He did not have an agreeable relationship with anyone, including us. My sister Elizabeth, her husband, and their two young children lived a few houses away from us. Joseph, his wife, and son lived next door within shouting distance, and had a chicken farm behind their home. My father still lived across the street in his self-made shack, which was caving in on him. He would stop by Joseph's to beg for eggs and other food items. Agnes was the most cordial to him, and gave him whatever he needed. I always wondered why she helped him out. Whether she was being a good Christian and trying to keep the peace, or being spiteful by doing something she knew goaded the rest of the family, I will never know.

I saw my father a lot; he came around our house too, as if my mother's absence had absolved him of his deeds. He was trying to get back into his own family's life and failing at it, miserably. My sisters never let him forget what he had done. He never apologized, and claimed he did not recall things being so awful, and that they were exaggerating and turning him into a monster. In fact, he felt that his children owed *him* an explanation for interfering in his relationship with *his* wife and ganging up on him.

When it came to my father, things were not that simple for me. Clearly, my siblings' feelings towards him were of hatred and nothing else, and they took advantage of every opportunity to express those feelings to him to his face. Of course, I had feelings of anger towards him too, but somehow, I still loved him. Honestly, I didn't know what my true feelings for him were. I did not feel quite right about ignoring him and yet, I felt having a relationship with him would be a betrayal against my entire family.

My exchanges with him were limited to, "Mornin', Dad," under my breath. I acknowledged him because he was my father. I had to steel myself against the pain I felt inside over not having a bond with him, but still, I could not forgive him. At first, he would respond to my greetings. However, when he would try to extend the conversations and start asking me questions, and I did not answer and just kept on walking, he got the message. Soon, he stopped responding to my greetings and stopped acknowledging me altogether. He knew that I was waiting to join my mother in the States, so he told neighbors that was why I was acting superior and rejecting him. Soon, all communication between us stopped. In his mind, because he had never laid a hand on me, I had no reason to rebuff his attempts. His alcohol-soaked brain could not comprehend that, although it was true that his physical and verbal brutality were not directed at me personally, his actions towards my mother and every one of my siblings, traumatized me. Even though I loved him because he was my father, I could not like him as a person.

My father was coming to the realization that he was on his own and completely alone. His four grandchildren had already heard stories about him, knew why he lived alone in a shack, and why his children didn't want anything to do with him. He didn't have any friends, and had outlived the few he previously had. Our father was trying to fix something that was permanently broken. He was aging and nobody cared about him. He was going to die alone and he knew it. His mother's words so many years ago had come to fruition. His family had turned on him.

During our last week in Saint Lucia, Elias and I said goodbye to friends and relatives, gave away some of our belongings, and packed just a few things in our two bags. My brother and I did not say goodbye to our father.

We didn't take very much with us because, after all, in America, clothes, money, and everything else you need grow on trees. Don't they? So, on a bright August morning in 1984, my brother and I left St. Lucia on an 8:30 a.m. American Airlines flight bound for JFK International Airport in New York City.

I was seventeen when my life in Saint Lucia ended and a promising new one in America began.

From Sea to Shining Sea

OUR MOVE TO AMERICA was a difficult transition for everyone. After living in the States for a year, my mother and Lawrence still had not adjusted to being in a new country. My Aunty Theresa had a scenario in her mind of how life would be, and how things should work, but without considering the needs of the four other people who would be living with her. She thought she would control everything, and that in our gratitude, we'd fall in line.

My aunt never married or lived with anyone before she found herself living in her one bedroom apartment with relatives she barely knew. She occupied her bedroom, my bothers slept in the living room, my mother and I shared a tiny alcove in the living room.

My aunt's landlord did not approve of us living in the apartment, and made his dissatisfaction obvious by insulting us every chance he got. He wasn't completely to blame though. It seems my aunt gave him no notice of our arrival, figuring he wouldn't allow more people in the small apartment, or raise her rent. He lived below us and we caused him grief. We forgot to lock the building's entrance door altogether or properly. We were noisy, not familiar with the rules of apartment living. Our first winter was brutal. We couldn't keep warm with the flimsy coats my aunt got us, so we kept the heat tuned up all day and all night. The heating bill, which was his responsibility, was sky high. Pissed, he harassed my aunt threatening to kick her out. If she was out, we were out!

By the time Elias and I arrived, the relationship between her, my mother, and Lawrence, was already tense. The winter's troubles, and two more people, only made matters worse. We tried being quiet and keep a low profile. This was very difficult, as having to unlock three doors, each with several locks, thwarted all attempts at quick and quite entries and departures. Unaccustomed to keys, we were constantly losing them and getting locked out of the building. Unfortunately, the landlord would witness our maladjustment. He would reluctantly let us back into the building, accompanied by a flood of insults. His request was always the same, "You, go back to your country!"

Theresa was particular about how she wanted things done and kept a tight rein on everything. She wanted the apartment kept neat at all times but with little closet space, that was troublesome. The four of us shared the living room space as a bedroom, yet we had to keep it looking and functioning like a living room. She liked rice cooked on Sundays, with a choice of beans or caned mixed vegetables. She did not tolerate waste of any kind, so we had to reheat and eat the same food all week until it was all consumed, which meant having rice for dinner almost every night.

We could only buy items on sale. Aunty bought nasty-looking expired meat because it was on clearance.

Empty yogurt cups were drinking cups. At first, we resisted, but she insisted, "A yogurt container is a ready-made cup. So, why would you risk breaking a glass?"

"Because that's what glasses are made for - drinking!" I often answered in my head. But we obliged, since it was her home, she made the rules.

We purchased only Bounty paper towels - the "quicker-picker-upper" were rinsed, hung and reused. Any broken china was a cause for embarrassing interrogation. She kept the only telephone in her closed bedroom. Lights and television were off at nine. There was no double flushing allowed. You completely finished your personal business before you flushed once, and only once. Anything more was accompanied by sounds and gestures of disapproval, or a lecture on waste.

"When you waste hot water or flush twice, you burn and flush my money!"

We had transferred to a new prison, one without vast fields to provide escape. Although my mother and Lawrence had secured jobs upon their arrival, their small salaries made it impossible to pay half my aunt's rent and save enough to move out.

It wasn't long after landing on the shores of America, that I realized the grass was not necessarily greener on this side of the Atlantic. In fact, there wasn't much green. There was a whole lot of gray concrete, unfriendliness, and fear. Oh yeah, New York City in the '80s was grimy, cold, and rough!

My mother hated almost everything about New York: her babysitting job, the cold weather, the inability to find her favorite Saint Lucian foods, the list went on. What she hated the most was the amount of freedom that American children had and their total lack of respect for their elders. The fact that the kids she babysat called her *Susanna* and not *Miss Susanna* or *Miss Joseph* drove her mad! She'd come home complaining, "I am *not* these kids' friend. Me, so old I can be their grandmother, and they call me

Suzanna! No respect!" She could not spank them, and therefore felt helpless, as she was no longer in charge or the authority figure. She found out that in America, kids had all sorts of rights. She was miserable and cried a lot—nothing new for my mother.

Aunt Theresa, unbeknownst to me, had already secured a live-in babysitter/housekeeper position for me somewhere in New Jersey. I had to take two trains and a bus to work. For someone who was used to fresh tropical breezes, the stinky, crowded subways, buses, and streets were disturbing. I would try holding my breath in order to protect my nasal passages from the stench of the dirty streets. That first summer was rough!

Upon arrival in New Jersey, my employers picked me up at the bus stop and took me to their house to clean, cook, and care for their young son and infant daughter. My salary was $100 a week, which was about what my mother was making. I went back to Brooklyn on weekends, but sometimes, according to my employer's plans, had to return earlier than usual on Sundays. Sometimes, I'd have to wait around late Saturdays until they dropped me off at the bus stop, only to return twenty-four hours later. The commute was killing me and I wanted to kill everybody else, then myself!

I was on autopilot. My unhappiness so profound, it was a throbbing physical sensation in my chest. At work, I never had my own room. Instead, I slept in the family room, where the kids played and watched TV. With no private time, I was constantly on duty. They were incapable of flushing the toilet after themselves, or doing any sort of housekeeping over the weekend. Trying to put that place back together again every Monday morning was like cleaning up in the aftermath of a war. It took me at least two days to put the house back in order. In between cleaning, laundry, and cooking, I was also completely responsible for two kids and all their needs. The man of the house, an accountant, worked out of the basement, so I never felt comfortable while working to listen to music or anything relaxing. Along with my household responsibilities, Mr. Steinberg often had me do odd jobs like help him clean up in the yard as he trimmed trees or help him carry bales of insulation up a ladder into the attic. After a couple of months, my sorry state had taken its toll.

One Saturday morning, without informing or seeking my aunt or mother's permission, I quit my job. I left a note for my employers on the kitchen table while Mr. Steinberg waited for me in the car to drive me to the bus station.

When I arrived home that night, I announced to the whole family that I had quit my job, but that they should not worry because I was going to get another one right away, one that would allow me to live at home. My aunt coughed a little and left the room. She returned with a shoebox and produced a ton of receipts detailing all the expenditures she had accumulated on our behalf. To our surprise, Theresa had maintained a meticulous record of every item she had purchased for us, for which she now expected repayment. Pronto!

"Well… young lady, if you think you can just quit one job and get another one right away, then you must be able to pay these bills that have been piling up and I've been trying to take care of all by myself. You think it's been easy taking care of you all? Well, it hasn't!"

At first, she was addressing me but soon started turning on everybody as she gave each of us a total, which was our individual responsibility. My brothers and I received bills for clothing, food, and toiletries. My mother received similar bills, along with all our pre-America expenses, visa and application fees. Nothing was unaccounted! Her condescending, sarcastic tone and actions were so mischievous. My mother did what she did best. She started sobbing.

The bombshell that we owed Theresa a great deal of money that we didn't have was the final straw. As my mother's sister and our aunt, we were under the impression that she was doing this out of the kindness of her heart. We were all appreciative of her and the sacrifices she made in order to give us a fresh start, and opportunities we would not have had otherwise. But, at that moment, we were not prepared for her shocker.

A huge argument ensued. My brothers started shouting at Theresa, while my mother cried. I was in a state of disbelief and felt guilty that my actions had started it.

Certainly, I would have stayed at my job if I knew I had to pay her back and so soon. Perhaps if my aunt had been frank from the beginning, and told us about the strenuous financial situation, I would have made different decisions and planned accordingly. We could have obtained second jobs, started looking for own place or other ways to lessen the burden we were placing on her.

Growing up, I wanted to believe only the Saint Lucian branch of my family tree was rotten. Since Theresa lived abroad and had managed to stay uninvolved in the ongoing land wars, I dared hope she was different. But in that instant, when she was standing in the living room/our bedroom in her flowered Muumuu, throwing all the things she had done for us back in our staggered faces, in that familiar vindictive manner, it was then I grasped it. My entire family tree was decayed.

I should have known better. While it is true Theresa had not taken part in the family altercations over the years in Saint Lucia, in the end though, she accepted her legal share, along with my mother's divided portion of land. Theresa, on principle, should have rejected the extra portion that did not belong to her. And even after accepting the land, she could've followed my uncle Gregra's guilt ridden example, returning his portion of my mother's property back to her. That day the proof was in, she was no different.

During all the fussing and shouting, my aunt stated the obvious. It was time for us to move out and find a place of our own.

A Place to Call Our Own

WITH LIMITED FUNDS FOR the required security deposit and first month's rent, and lack of references, we soon discovered that our apartment choices were narrow and few. Landlords with nice houses were not willing to take a chance on newbie tenants. Fortunately, on our third day of constant house hunting, we found someone willing to give us a chance.

We crammed our few belongings into two taxicabs and moved to our new home the following day. The reason we got the apartment was clear: no sane family would choose to move into that building. The apartment was on DeKalb Avenue, one of the worst sections of the Bedford Stuyvesant area in Brooklyn. In the 1980s, that neighborhood was notorious for its high levels of violence and crime. Contaminated with drugs of all kinds, it seemed like everyone on our block was involved in the drug trade, either taking or selling it. Gang activity and shootouts were common occurrences. Most of the buildings were dilapidated and/or abandoned burned out shells. Most of the doors and windows in buildings were broken or boarded-up, including in our building. Our apartment building was under complete renovation, by the aging owner all by himself, while tenants were living there. The paint was completely faded. Light fixtures were hanging by exposed electrical wiring that ran all over the place and a broken wooden stairway lead to our second floor apartment. There were no doorbells or intercom system.

The only good thing about our new home was the sizable living space. It had three bedrooms, a living room, dining room, eat-in kitchen, and bathroom. My brothers and I each chose a bedroom, and turned the dining room into a bedroom for our mother. Our new financial arrangement was that my two brothers and I would share the rent, utilities, and other household operating expenses equally, with telephone and other personal bills paid by the responsible party. We agreed that our mother should save her meager salary for her intended return to Saint Lucia.

Within a week of leaving my job and moving to the new apartment, I obtained a job as a cashier at a Duane Reade drug store in Manhattan. Getting another job so soon on my own, gave me the confidence I needed to handle another situation I had wanted to take care of for some time.

For too long, I had heard my mother praising the virtues of virginity. Yet another burden placed on me as a girl, and I was sick of it. This would be my choice, done on my terms. I would pick whom, when, and where. I was ready.

The assistant manager, at the Duane Reade store where I worked, was a gentle, mild-mannered man of Indian decent with a charming accent. I'm not sure why I chose this particular guy, and right now, I can't even remember his name, but something about him got my attention. Maybe it was because he reminded me of my godfather.

One Friday night after work as we hurried to the train station, I asked him to the movies the following evening. He accepted, I asked for his address and told him I would meet him at his apartment since it was on our way to the movie theater. That summer evening I carefully dressed, making sure that I shaved and had matching bra and panties. I dabbed a little perfume in all the right places and told my family I was going to the movies with friends from work, and took the train from Brooklyn to the Bronx.

I buzzed at the front door of the two-family house where he lived. He led me upstairs to his apartment and told me to wait as he finished getting dressed. I wandered casually into his bedroom, making small talk.

We would neither be seeing a movie or have dinner. I was on a mission.

By then, my body language had made it quite clear why I came. It didn't take much convincing; he was an accommodating host.

The matter was an experience in awkwardness. We were both inexperienced and had trouble using the condom. He was clumsy, eager, and in a hurry, and me not enjoying any of it. The only thing I took pleasure in that night was running my fingers through his soft curly hair. The entire affair lasted a few minutes. It was all I needed, the deed was done. I kissed him on the lips, said goodnight, and left.

On Monday when we saw each other at work, we acted as if nothing had happened. He did, however begin to show me some preferential treatment and that was nice. We never talked about what transpired nor did we socialize outside of work ever again.

By this time, I no longer believed in God, fairy tales, handsome princes on white horses, or heroes coming to save me. I had to take care of me. Ending my virginity was no big deal - just another chore I could now place a check mark next to on my to do list. During that time, I got my GED. My Saint Lucia high school diploma wasn't recognized by the Board of Education. I took classes in restaurant management, which came in handy, because after a few months of working at the drugstore, I lost my job for failing my first polygraph test. I had no clue what a polygraph test was, or that mandatory testing was a violation of employee rights. Duane Reade management did not explain what was going on or what to expect. Strapped to a machine and questioned, unsure what to do, or how to answer the questions, I did my best to answer truthfully. I was petrified and nervous, which I suppose indicated guilt. They fired me and I was humiliated.

After losing that job, I moved from one meaningless, dissatisfying restaurant job to another as coffee maker, cashier, waitress or hostess. I did not mind working, as I had bills to pay. After completing a course in restaurant management, I received a promotion at my job. I became assistant manager at a restaurant on West 33rd Street in Manhattan, where I had been working for several months.

For a while, things were fine in our new household. However, tensions started developing again, when, with every passing month, Elias could not keep his end of our agreement. He could not hold down a job, yet he continued to call his girlfriend in Saint Lucia and couldn't pay the huge telephone bills.

No one really knew if Elias had a job or not. We knew he was being dishonest. He claimed he was working, but never had any money to contribute to the household like the rest of us were. Lawrence and I always had to cover his portion from our small paychecks. Often forced to pay his bills or face having our telephone disconnected, we were riled with Elias' irresponsibility. Lawrence, incapable of resolving conflicts in any other fashion, continued the bullying behavior he had practiced back in Saint Lucia. Now adults, we should be handling our troubles as civilized grown-ups. But Lawrence had not changed, and was still willing to make use of his fists.

Elias and Lawrence were persistently at each other's throats, usually with me trying to keep the peace. Our mother would lock herself in her room crying and praying. She had lost all power and authority and had no say in what we did. If we had boyfriends or girlfriends stay over, she would sulk and just go to her room, choking down the opinion she could not express, counting the days until her return back to Saint Lucia.

As Elias continued his irresponsible behavior, Lawrence remained the proverbial intimidator. At that point, Elias had grown bigger, taller, and stronger than Lawrence. Lawrence could no longer push Elias around the way he did in the past, and he was having trouble accepting that, so he kept trying. The fighting would get so bad between them that the police often had to intervene.

During that time, I was dating Tony, one of my supervisors at work. We would go in to work together sometimes, but kept our relationship a secret from co-workers. I would walk in through the employee entrance while he went through the front entrance. Tony would let me take longer breaks without anyone noticing. At times, when I was running late, he would cover for me. I had an ally, someone looking out for me, what a refreshing experience.

After two years of us living together, things came to a screeching halt one afternoon. This time, the fight involved all three of us. Lawrence moved his girlfriend in without consulting the rest of us. This woman's talents involved sleeping, eating, and satisfying Lawrence's sexual needs. She lounged around the house all day in her sleepwear like a permanent guest, not cleaning up after herself. After about a month of that behavior, the rest of us had enough. I didn't mind Lawrence's girlfriend staying at the house, after all, we had our own rooms. What I could not tolerate was someone not willing to pull their weight and pitch in to help maintain the household. We left one of her dirty dishes sitting in the sink for a week before we confronted Lawrence about our dissatisfaction. As expected, he did not appreciate it.

"Well, your boyfriend is living here too!" Lawrence rebuked, pointing at me.

Before I could respond, Elias stepped in. "That's different. At least, they asked if he could move in. And he cooks. He even painted the bathroom for us. He pitches in."

"And he *has* a job and isn't sleeping *all* day long!" I added.

Lawrence didn't care that we were making sense. Rational thinking made Lawrence dizzy, so he became enraged. He proceeded to inform us that since everything in the house belonged to him and if we did not like the living situation, we should consider moving out. When the distasteful matter was over and the dust had settled, our mother decided she'd had enough, and two weeks later, she moved back to Saint Lucia. I moved to a dreadful apartment in the building next door, owned by our landlord, while Elias moved to a small room in an apartment building a few blocks away.

My one-bedroom apartment was a foot away from a drug house. Dealers could have easily stepped into my apartment, while getting away from the police or each other. Empty holes with no glass served as windows. Tony and I painted the place, covered the windows with cardboard decorating them with curtains. I bought some cheap carpets to cover the old, splintering wooden floors. Although the lease was in my name, Tony kind of thought it was his too. That lasted about a month. He refused to help with rent, and sometimes didn't show up for days. One weekend while he was away I packed all his stuff and left it outside the door, and changed the locks.

Lawrence, Elias, and I did not speak to for many years after that fight. I was fine with that. For all of the twenty years of my life, all I ever wanted was to get away from the madness. Although my apartment was a dump, it was all mine!

By Any Means Necessary

ALONE, AND ON MY own at last, I tried fashioning a new life. Determined to forget my past and forge forward. My life was my own; I could make whatever I wanted of it. Create the life I had dreamed and promised myself—the kind I deserved but never had.

Along with having a job in Manhattan, I spent all my free time there taking evening and weekend classes. I aimed to be an actress, so I took acting, and singing lessons. I attended accent reduction classes in an effort to lose my accent, which my acting teachers warned would prevent me from achieving my dream of fame.

One Saturday afternoon, armed with my daily cup of carrot juice, I stepped into the elevator at the Ed Sullivan Studios for my singing lessons. When the sweetest smile and kindest eyes greeted me, I returned the elevator operator's shy smile with a one of my own. To his look of curiosity at the vile-looking drink in my hand, I responded, "Carrot juice. It's not as bad as it looks." The elevator doors opened and I stepped out.

On my way out the building, I saw the elevator operator eating a slice of pizza.

"Having a late lunch?"

Through a mouthful of cheesy sauce, he mumbled pleasantries. I noticed he had an unfamiliar accent.

"Where you from?" I quipped.

"Just landed from Ireland. You some sort of professional singer?"

"I wish." I laughed, flattered. "Just taking classes."

"Where you from?" He persisted without much pause.

"Saint Lucia. Do you know where that is?" I questioned, since few people knew of my island, or its location.

"No." he answered, a little self-conscious.

"It's a tiny Caribbean island; close to Jamaica." I offered.

He glanced at his watch indicating he needed to return to work, so I took my chance on the gentle brown-eyed, blonde pony-tailed Irishman.

"By the way, I'm Esther. If you want to go out sometime, here's my number." I pulled out a pen and paper and wrote down my phone number.

As I wrote he said, "I'm Declan. I live in the Bronx and I'm still learning my away around."

"Well, in that case we can meet here on a Saturday and do something after you're done with work." I suggested as I rushed off not wanting to seem desperate.

A few days later, he called to say hello and asked me out the upcoming Saturday evening. After Declan finished work, we went to see *Lean on Me* starring Morgan Freeman. After the movie, we stopped for appetizers and drinks at Houlihan's.

I enjoyed hearing about Ireland and his experiences growing up there.

I felt safe with him; there was easiness in our interaction. He was impressed that I had my own place and plans for my future. I liked his gentle demeanor.

I asked him to come to Brooklyn with me. He accepted. Our date was becoming a night of "firsts" for Declan. He had never been to Brooklyn, or dated a black girl before.

After two years of living in Bedford Stuyvesant, stepping over vacant cocaine vials, and having my purse snatched from me more times than I cared to count, I had enough. It would've been easier for me to just stand on the street corner and hand my cash out to whoever wanted it. It would've saved me some heart-stopping moments—not to mention the time and money spent on having to replace my wallet, and identification. I was desperate to dump my dump of an apartment.

A move to Manhattan would be convenient and safer. But as an assistant manager at a small restaurant, I could not afford Manhattan rent. My co-worker Sandra and I decided to look for an apartment together. We found a decent, reasonably priced two-bedroom just a ten-minute walk from work. We paid the required one-month security deposit, and first months' rent and were all set to move in. On move-in day, my roommate called to inform me that a family emergency prevents her moving to the apartment and she had to back out of our arrangement. She was willing to forfeit her deposit so I could find another roommate. I needed to secure a new roommate immediately.

I called Declan in a panic. I told him my predicament, and asked if he wanted to be my roommate. Declan's apartment was like a hostel, every new Irish person who needed a temporary home ended up staying there. At first, he was fine with the crowd since he liked being surrounded by his fellow countrymen. He enjoyed drinking with them, and the money he was saving by sharing rent with so many people came in handy. But he knew that sooner or later, he would have to find a less hectic place to live.

I told him that there was no time like the present. I reminded Declan that since he worked late shifts, he needed a shorter and safer commute to and from work. I explained, "The new apartment will be perfect for you. It's only a few blocks from your work and besides," I continued, "we spend so much time together anyway, now we can spend all our free time together. Wouldn't that be nice?" It did not take much more persuading. He agreed to move in with me.

After only a few dates in about a month, Declan, and I set up house.

The romantic part of our relationship did not last long. However, the living situation was convenient, so we remained roommates. Like my previous boyfriends, I chose Declan because of his meek disposition, and while initially this quality made me feel safe, eventually I ended up hating and ridiculing them for it. Traits like tenderness were more like weaknesses to me. Part of me admired and wanted the calmness they offered, while subconsciously, I sought the lunacy I was accustomed to.

Our relationship did not stand a chance. We were from two completely different worlds. Moreover, being an interracial couple in the '80s and early '90s was dangerous.

During that period, Spike Lee was the up-and-coming director stirring up the already bubbling racial tensions with movies like *Do the Right Thing, Jungle Fever,* and *Malcolm X.* Declan and I went to see *Malcolm X* together one evening. Declan was the only white guy in the theatre, as it was filled with mostly African-American men getting riled by Malcolm X's speeches, about retribution against white people. He was encouraging black people to rise up and claim their freedom by any means necessary.

As we exited the theatre, five black young men surrounded us on the escalator, ogling us menacingly while repeating Malcolm X chant, "By any means necessary! By any means necessary!" There were five angry black men and just the two of us, Declan and I looked at each other, eyes filled with fear. We were certain they were going to assault. When we got to the theatre's lower level, there were more people, so we quickly disappeared among the crowd.

When in public, we made a conscious effort not to hold hands or show any signs of affection. Many times, we tried to walk as if we were strangers. But openly walking next to each other caused a response. The white folks gave us the looks, the African-Americans—both men and women—were vile. They spat and cursed at us. The black men would approach Declan

MEMORIES OF HELL, VISIONS OF HEAVEN • 91

wanting to fight him. He resisted, and would not say a word. I wanted to fight back. Declan didn't understand why I wanted to stoop to their level. The women would say things like, "Mmm, mmm, mmm! Do you *smell* something? It stinks around here." Then they would spit in our direction. Not used to such public displays and confrontations, those public spectacles freaked Declan out, but were right up my alley, and fueled me up. Reawakening and feeding my dormant demons. Violence was creeping back into my life and it did not take much for me to push back whenever threatened, mainly with fighting words. So I did what I do best.

For the first time in my life, I seriously considered getting a gun. When these unpleasant incidents occurred, I would get so excited and out of control and would say things like, "Damn, if only I had a gun, I would shoot those SOB's!" And I meant it.

I think Declan was scared more by my reactions than by what these ignorant people were saying and thought my need for retaliation was going to get us both killed.

We could not go out and have an enjoyable time together, although we liked each other, It was clear we could not be a couple.

While we were living together, Declan held a couple jobs. He worked double shifts as a security guard, and also worked at an irrigation company, installing automatic sprinkler watering systems on terraces, rooftops, and outdoor gardens in Manhattan. His aging boss at the irrigation company offered to sell Declan the company so he could retire. With my enthusiastic encouragement and promise of support, Declan purchased the company. I took on the financial responsibilities of the household, so he could save up the money to purchase the business.

Shortly after acquiring the company, Declan and I quit our jobs and I gave up my classes. We collaborated to turn our investment into a successful company. We did not have money to hire employees, so together we ran every aspect of the business. Declan, with my assistance, did the system installations and I paid attention to the billing and office side of the operation. Luckily, we were the only company offering system installations and maintenance in the Manhattan area at the time. With little competition, we soon had a solid client base. The work was grueling but it was satisfying being our own bosses and doing something new and different. With hard work and long hours, the business grew quickly, and we were able to hire a few employees and purchase a truck.

The more employees we hired, the more clients we gained, the more money we made, the unhappier I became. I convinced myself that money was what I always wanted. I shopped and spent money in an effort to quell the voices of discontent in my head.

In my pursuit of monetary and business success, I lost sight of my dreams, of becoming an actress, and furthering my education. I was distracted by financial achievement and too exhausted to engage in any of the activities that once brought me contentment. I could no longer deny my misery; still, I lacked the will to do anything about it. For fifteen more years, I would labor at the company, spinning my wheels like a pet hamster in my self-imposed cage.

The Name Game

CHRISTENED ESTHER JOSEPH, MY name became just another weapon in my mother's arsenal against me. As a newly converted Pentecostal, my mother learned of the tale told in the book of Esther.

The story chronicles the selfless and noble act of a young queen named Esther who risked her life to save her people. When Esther learned of a plot that would exterminate her entire tribe, she single-handedly devised a plan that swayed the heart of her husband the king, saving them from certain death.

My mother fell in love with the virtuous queen and came up with the notion that since my name was also Esther then I should become the modern version of my namesake.

Those were standards I had no way of living up to. Whenever I did something wrong that she reckoned required a beating, she would chastise me further by making comments like, "You don't deserve your name. Queen Esther would never have done anything so sinful!" or, "Shame, shame, what would Queen Esther say? She would be so ashamed of you right now."

I suppose, after a few such whippings I began to dislike my name. Why did I have the same name, and be compared to someone I could never be like? She has a whole book in the Bible named after her for Pete's sake; that's a lot of pressure for a kid!

While receiving a spanking one day, I swore that as soon as I was old enough, my first act of emancipation would be to change my name.

***

In 1992, my discontent was irrefutable. Restless and dissatisfied with my life in the States, I contemplated moving to another country.

In my youth, I had learned of Saint Lucia's French connection and had always wanted to explore that link—so I decided the time was perfect for a trip to Paris.

The minute I arrived, I fell in love with the city. I liked Paris better than New York for many reasons. I became fond of how Parisians made rudeness chic. New Yorkers on the other hand, were just plain rude and aggressive. In Paris, I never heard anyone threaten to beat someone for accidentally bumping into them, or sat in a seat on a train or bus they deemed theirs. I never witnessed a public dispute on the streets of Paris, which was commonplace in New York City. I was immediately enchanted by the Parisian leisurely lifestyle and by how meals and lunch breaks was respected and savored.

One delightful mid-afternoon, I was having coffee at a street side café near the Louvre when I sampled the sweetest, creamiest, most scrumptious cheese ever. In broken French, I inquired about it.

"Brie, Madam, made here, local," the waiter responded.

While reveling in the deliciousness of the cheese's flavor, I looked around the café and noticed that others were enjoying it too. Then a thought entered my head. This cheese is everything I should be! Sweet, soft, liked and appreciated for these qualities. In a moment of strange naïveté, I reasoned that if I took on the name of the cheese then maybe I would also take on its characteristics.

That day I decided to give myself the gift I promised myself years before. I started introducing and referring to myself as Brie Joseph. I was BJ to my friends, which was shorter and even sweeter.

Back in the United States, the desire to become a milder and cuter me, proved more difficult than I imagined, and I soon became bored with trying. By 1993, my life was snowballing into a righteous mess.

Declan and I were still business partners, working many long hours, so we rented large spaces, which we divided into shared office and living space, and our private bedrooms. Because of the nature of our business, we often had late night emergency calls. This meant that we went out in the middle of the night to attend to broken pipes and other water and flooding issues. Therefore, living and working in the same space was a convenient and effective way to run the business.

Living in the same space—not as a couple, but as the company operators —made our personal lives messy and tense. Even though we weren't involved as a couple anymore, jealousy was always in the air, either from Declan or from those we were dating. In my convoluted mind, the living arrangement was fine and made good sense. I was undoubtedly not in love with Declan, but others had issues with us living together after having been a romantic couple. I could not understand why they could not see or accept the practicality of our living arrangement and let it go. So, I stopped dating.

As time went on, we no longer had to take care of everything ourselves. Therefore, Declan and I were able to move to separate apartments within walking distance to the office.

I should have been thrilled; I had a nice apartment and the business was moving along smoothly. Yet, I could not shake my unwavering sense of emptiness and longing.

I was incapable of establishing close connections with anyone; not even Declan, estranged from my mother and most of my siblings. Lawrence and Elias were still in the States, but we still had no contact. After months of not hearing from me, Francisca would call to see if I was still alive. While I appreciated her efforts at trying to maintain a relationship, our conversations always led to updates on the family, which always brought up the bad memories I was trying to forget. I didn't look forward to our telephone conversations, as they always left me in an awful condition. I would fall into a deep depression, which took weeks to wrest.

Those heavy black phases were like having two inebriated idiots inside my head engaging in non-stop, nonsensical dialogue and sacks of bricks in my chest and stomach. The voices made my head ache all the time, and the pressure in my heart area was so heavy and dull that I felt little sensation in that region of my body. I hungered for relief from my debilitating agonies.

Music gave me some solace. At the time, I never understood my fascination with ABBA's music. But slowly I started to understand the bizarre link and logic. Music always had the ability to take me away from my painful circumstances as a child. Now an adult, it was doing the opposite. Taking me back to my childhood, returning gave me the opportunity to grieve an unknown loss. Now, I was finally expressing my grief by crying obsessively. I now understood the damage done and what I had been denied. That knowledge hurt deeper than living through it. "Dancing Queen" was the one song that, as a teen, had resonated so acutely, but smothered by my mother's heavy-handedness. Now only grief and deep yearning remained attached to a song that was once my cry for freedom.

In my apartment, my precious dog Bridges as the only witness, I played that song over and over, and wept for days until I had no more tears. During those scenes, Bridges knew intuitively what to do. He did not try to engage or distract me, but unconditionally sat close, watching me intently. With compassion in his eyes, he was trying to tell me something. It took several of these episodes before I realized he was trying to communicate to me that better days were ahead and that he would stay by my side until we got through this together. I held on to his hundred-pound body night after lonely night - his presence was my only comfort. Some how, this shedding of tears became a regular form of purging, the only released from some of the confusion and heaviness that plagued my soul.

My inability to enjoy the things I had fed my resentment and cynicism, which I directed at everyone. I could not maintain a relationship with a man for more than a couple of weeks, nor cultivate or handle friendships with women. My dark disposition erected such a thick wall that no good or decent person would have any interest penetrating—but was a magnet for losers and cheaters. How could I possibly attract anything else?

I was often being dumped or doing the dumping. If someone nice did fall through the cracks, I didn't know what to do. Something must be wrong with him I thought, and run in the opposite direction. When the crazies came around, I knew in my heart that I no longer wanted that in my life. It was a no-win situation and an awful way to live.

One afternoon lying in bed, crippled by thoughts of self-pity, it dawned on me that my new name had betrayed me. Plainly, the optimistic, positive feelings I had when I decided to rename myself Brie had melted like cheap cheese left laying about, forgotten. I was a pile of trash on a Manhattan sidewalk on a hot summer day. I was garbage.

During that time, I was in the process of becoming a U.S. citizen. The citizenship application gave allowances for name changes, I seized the opportunity and once again change my name, this time I legally became Debrie Joseph.

The High Cost of Lust

BY THE MID-NINETIES, I was traveling a lot more, to Saint Lucia mostly. I never understood why I kept going back there, as the trips were always the same. I was still harboring lots of bitterness and ill will towards my family. Yet out of a misguided sense of responsibility, I would over-spend on tons of gifts. I was successful and wanted to share nice things with them. Essentially, I was trying to buy their love and approval.

My trips always started with a sense of promise and excitement; expecting that this time, they would accept me and offer some type of apology for their appalling behavior towards me as a child. But mostly, I was seeking affection from my mother, or at least have her say that she was proud of me for being hard working and having made something of my life. Any of these things would have brought me some satisfaction.

Nothing new happened and my trips ended in disappointment. Never happy with what was going on during the visit, I would dredge up the past. As quickly as I brought up the subject, I was ignored and accused of making up stories. I was seeking reconciliation, but my family was not even willing to meet me halfway. They refused to acknowledge that we all played a role in what happened and the hurt that remained. They chose rather, to place all the blame on our father, when in fact, we all had a function in that saga. They couldn't see that. Perhaps to acknowledge any accountability would somehow unwillingly diminish their right to hate him so much. Then they might have had to admit that maybe there had been other solutions to dealing with our father. They just could not accept that.

It was on one of my trips to Saint Lucia that I met my last serious boy-friend. There he was, on my connecting flight from Puerto Rico to Saint Lucia, two rows ahead to the left. He was perfect. He had a military-style haircut, gentle features, and a laid-back way about him. He was wearing a colorful plaid shirt, his attempt at suitable island attire. It was a big contrast to his blonde hair and very light skin. He was chatting excitedly with his group. As I eavesdropped, I learned that they were on their way to saving the world. He was soft-spoken with a tender smile and laugh. Between the three-hour flight and airport check-out, I managed to introduce myself, slip him my mother's phone number in Saint Lucia where I would be staying, and elicit a sincere promise that he would call as soon as he could. I was in lust. This may turn into a very exciting vacation after all, I thought.

Dennis was a member of a small group of United States Peace Corps volunteers heading to the Caribbean as a form of cultural exchange between the U.S. and the Caribbean Islands. These American volunteers committed to a period of two years to teach, and perform other social duties in schools and other institutions in poor Caribbean countries. As fortune would have it, at the time, the Peace Corps Caribbean headquarters was stationed in Saint Lucia. And, although the volunteers would be assigned to several of the other Islands, all volunteers were initially sent to Saint Lucia for two weeks of training. They stayed with local host families, who the government paid to house, feed, and give these young Americans a crash course in Caribbean living, etiquette, and culture.

Two days after our airport meeting, Dennis and I met again. This time he was a guest at my mother's house! Unbeknownst to me, my mother was a host mother, a head host mother at that, and as such, it was her responsibility to host the welcoming get-together for the volunteers and their host families. Dennis was staying with a family in the city.

During our conversation that night, I learned that he was twenty-five years old, from Cincinnati, Ohio with a degree in Art History. Dennis too was from a broken family; his father had abandoned his family when he was a boy. He had four brothers and a sister and was of German-Irish decent. He revealed that his motives for joining the Peace Corps had not been purely altruistic. Dennis, not unlike many other volunteers who join the Peace Corps, unable to find good paying jobs and repay their mounting student loan bills, became Peace Corps workers. In doing so, their loans can be deferred or absolved by the U.S. Government.

For two weeks, we were inseparable - spending every second of his free time together. We nightclub hopped until the wee hours of the morning; shared long late night strolls on the beach; and made passionate love in the dark under tall coconut trees, while the summer breeze cooled our hot skin. It was intoxicating. I was receiving attention and admiration and he was having fun with an Americanized island native. Dennis said that he "didn't feel so lost or alone having an Island Girl as his guide who understood his American ways." My family, including my mother, liked him and he was great with my young nieces and nephews. Dennis had an infectious, child-like quality that endeared us all to him.

The day before Dennis left for the Island of Saint Kitts, I returned to the United States. Love letters and long expensive telephone calls followed our separation, and as soon as he settled into his assigned rent-free apartment, I made my first visit.

I visited Dennis three times during his first year in Saint Kitts. He was not making any money, so when I visited, I'd splurge on extravagant activities: island-hopping, staying at the best hotels, and dining at fancy restaurants. We enjoyed every minute of our limited time together. I also became friends with the other volunteers stationed on Saint Kitts.

The small circle of volunteers knew that Dennis was having an affair with his Venezuelan Spanish teacher. He admitted the affair to me, probably because he knew I would find out through our mutual friends anyway.

I forgave him for a number of reasons. First, he admitted the indiscretion to me and that was commendable enough. Thousands of miles separated us, and it was unreasonable to expect loyalty from him. More to the point, I didn't believe men were capable of fidelity. On my end, I needed his interest, as without his attention my life was an empty series of days with nothing but work to keep me going. The thought of someone caring and looking forward to my visits kept melancholy at bay. In many ways, I was becoming my mother, the long-suffering spouse. Dennis wasn't beating me, but by allowing me to take on the financial burden of the relationship, and by not being faithful he was taking advantage of me.

I knew no other way to show love but through monetary things. The gifts and money I was spending were my way of expressing my love for him. My efforts will make him love me back, I thought.

Still, my expensive, shallow attempts at immediate gratification did not reap the rewards I hoped. There I was carrying the entire weight of our relationship, aware of it, yet I could not stop myself. Since I chose to continue, I should've been able to enjoy the nice places and wonderful things we were doing. But I couldn't.

Whenever we were having a good time, I always expected something to put a damper on it, so I prepared myself for the unpleasantness I was sure would come. I even tried to expedite it. I would bring up the money, the cheating issue, or his ex-girlfriend, anything to create an argument.

Dennis never argued back. Most times, he would just walk away annoyed and embarrassed. And that was enough to take away the "good time" feeling we were having. When he did respond, it was something like, "Well, this was your idea," or, "I didn't ask you spend all this money."

"You could've refused to come or talked me out of it. You always get more excited about going than I do. It seemed like a good idea at the time, now I know better." Rolling my eyes, I'd continue, "A *real* man would find a way to contribute something."

I was never interested in his rationalizations. I was just looking for a fight. But, I continued with Dennis—plus the vacation sex was great.

Dennis did not complete his two-year assignment. He resigned from the Peace Corps after the first year and returned to Ohio. So my trips switched from Saint Kitts to Cincinnati. I fell immediately in love with his family, especially his mother and his younger twin brothers. They liked me too. On the outside, it seemed like I had it all together. His mother thought that as a successful businesswoman, I would be a good influence on her "can't commit to anything" son.

I appreciated his mother's maternal efforts; her life revolved around caring for and supporting her children. His twin brothers made me feel like I was part of the family, since they were both involved in interracial relationships. I felt very comfortable and at home with them; and admired the fact that they worked for Amnesty International, a human rights organization.

For another year and a half, Dennis and I continued in a long distance relationship. This long distance thing was great; having someone special in my life but not having to deal with them on a daily basis was ideal. I called, or took his phone calls, only when I wanted to, and was in the mood to talk. I was the one in control; I was the one who traveled to see him. I saw those trips as vacations from my life and I always had a good time. The family setting kept things low-key and minimized our disagreements.

In Cincinnati, we didn't stay in fancy hotels, but in his mother's basement, where he lived. We went out to bars and hung out with his brothers at sporting events. During the last few trips, tension started to build. I questioned where the relationship was headed and again, complained about how I was still the one spending all the money to keep it going. He was a moocher and a mama's boy—two things that doom men's relationships with women.

Our last argument and a possible business opportunity impelled Dennis to move to New York. Perhaps, he also came because he loved me. He moved in with me into my studio apartment. His "opportunity" was a pyramid scheme that brought him no fortune, only more debt.

After a few months and when realities sank in, Dennis become disillusioned and depressed. In an effort to lift our spirits and resuscitate our relationship, we decided to go back to the fantasy that had been our entire relationship before we moved in together. We tried forgetting our problems, and fall in love all over again by planning a trip to the ultimate fantasy city. We spent two months in Paris, as I was still entertaining the idea of moving there.

Along with all the sightseeing, dancing, eating, and enjoying everything the "City of Lights" had to offer, I took concrete steps towards making plans. I visited schools in the hopes of studying there. I also looked at apartments, or as the Europeans call them—flats, to figure out how much it would cost to live there. A lot!

Again, it was all on me. When we returned from Paris, I was completely exhausted from carrying the weight of two people, and serious arguments occurred more often. My anger was out of control; I was getting into the habit of smashing and throwing things. I was putting into practice the things I learned from my parents and siblings.

On our last evening together, we were in bed arguing. I physically kicked Dennis out of bed and onto the hard wood floor, flat on his back. After getting up, I could tell he was hurt. I will never forget the look in Dennis' eyes when he said, "I love you, but I can't be with you."

He left in the middle of the night and returned the next day to pick up his belongings. He didn't even look or talk to me. He moved back home to his mama soon after.

Until then, I knew somewhere deep inside that I deserved love, and had refused to give in to believing the unkind words my mother had said to me over the years. Although she never actually said, *I don't love you*, or, *you do not deserve my love*, her actions conveyed those messages quite clearly, forcing me to accept the scrapings of my father's affections.

After all, I first accepted my dad's weird love, but later rejected it because I knew I deserved better. The years I spent improving myself, pursuing acting, and growing a business assured me that I was right, and had enabled me to build up a little self-esteem and confidence—things I never had before. I spent many years trying to prove my family wrong. I knew I'd earned all the things I was working for and had achieved. However, the end of my relationship with Dennis made it seem that my mother might be right after all: no man would want me. It destroyed everything good I felt about myself.

Of all the boyfriends I had, Dennis was the one I fell for the hardest. He was the first and only man to take me home to meet his family. Maybe the idea of being part of a supportive family was what I fell in love with. Initially, that was one of the reasons I fought so desperately to salvage our relationship. Either way, he cared enough to relocate and welcomed me into his family. However, in the end he was unable to stand with and love me for who I was—me. He didn't want to try to work through our problems as a couple. And if he couldn't love me enough to do that, then who would?

A "Raydio" of Hope

PARALYZED WITH FEAR AND an overwhelming feeling of worthless-
ness after Dennis' departure, I could not eat, work, or sleep. I found conso-
lation only in thoughts of death and how brave it would be if only I
could go through with killing myself. I just wanted to stop the continuous
pain, and thought that putting an end to it all was the only way to do so. I
had the distorted belief that those who could take their lives were coura-
geous, and that they were making a conscious and deliberate choice. I on
the other hand, was a coward who couldn't help herself.

I spent days lying in bed contemplating the different ways I could
commit suicide: leaping off my eighteen-story apartment building, getting
drunk and slitting my wrists with a blade in the bath, swallowing a bottle of
sleeping pills, and the most plausible and effective, jumping onto subway
tracks as a train was approaching. I was convinced no one would miss me
when I was gone. I was scared of everything, the silence—my own thoughts
—often keeping the TV and radio on at the same just to keep them at bay.

One weekday, after not showering, changing my clothes, or going to
work for three days, I laid in bed crying. Again, I had the radio tuned into
public radio, when a call-in program came on. The therapist host took calls
from listeners and tried to solve their issues in about thirty seconds. The
therapist's non-judgmental and rational style impressed me.

Like most people of my culture, I did not believe in psychotherapy nor
considered it. What good would telling my problems to a total stranger
achieve? Furthermore, my mother would regard this as revealing personal
business. In addition, I knew the gravity of my situation and the power my
inner demons had over me. My psychological issues were complex and I
believed I was out of options.

As much as I would have been content enough to spend the rest of my
life in bed, I knew I couldn't. And since I lacked the nerve to end my life, I
had to do something. Seeking treatment had not entered my head until
then. In that moment of hope, I realized that I needed the assistance of a
heavy-duty professional, and that if anyone was equipped to help me, it was
that therapist. At the end of the show when the therapist's office telephone
number was broadcast, I wrote it down and made the call right away. I

didn't give myself the chance to talk myself out of doing it. If I had waited one more second, I would not have made that call.

Since that therapist was so popular, the receptionist said that I might have to wait weeks to get an appointment to see him. But luckily, at the moment of my call, a cancellation had just come through and I took the available spot. I had an appointment for the following Monday morning, less than a week away.

My Name is Star

THE RADIO HOST/THERAPIST WELCOMED me into his lavishly decorated office and asked why I felt I needed therapy.

Without hesitation, I boldly exclaimed, "My life is shit. I'm going insane. The negative thoughts won't go away. I just want them to stop. Better yet, I want to die. And if you don't help me now, I will do something awful." I had been waiting a week to say this.

"Okay, well, based on what you've just told me, I have a perfect match for you. I'm going to call her in so you ladies can get to know each and schedule your sessions together."

"Oh, no! I came here so *you* could help me. I do not want to see anyone else. If anyone can help me, it's you. I *will not* accept anyone else."

"Sorry, I'm retired. I don't take on clients anymore. I match patients with the therapists that can best help them, Don't worry, everyone here is expertly qualified to help you."

"Well, if you won't help me, then there's nothing more to talk about,"

I said, as I snatched my handbag, stood up and headed for the door. There was a reason I came here and that hope was sailing off, a life preserver floating away from the fingers of a drowning woman.

"Wait a minute, Ms. Joseph. Please, sit down, he said pointing to the chair I'd just vacated. I flopped back into the chair and waited in impatient silence, he too was silent, trying to figuring things out in his head.

Finally, he said, "I'm a very busy man with lots of other responsibilities. And I wouldn't normally do this, but I'll make an exception. I'll help you, but you must agree to my conditions."

He explained the rules of his therapy: I needed to cancel appointments at least twenty-four hours in advance or I would still be charged for the session; I couldn't quit no matter how tough things got; and I needed to follow his recommendations to the letter. I happily agreed.

For the first month I was hopeful, as I felt I was heading in the right direction.

During our first few appointments, he asked about my upbringing, my experiences as a child growing up and about my name. "Debrie? What's that about?" Intuitively, he knew that was not my given name.

"I was baptized *Esther*. I detest that name. Do you know the biblical story?"

"I think so, Esther the queen?" He inquired.

"Right."

I explained and that whenever my mother would beat me up; she made a point of telling me how undeserving I was of such a righteous name. I told him how I'd promised myself to get rid of that name the first chance I got. I shared the story of my travels, and my fist trip to Paris—how I fell in love with brie, and renamed myself after the cheese. He could not keep a straight face and chuckled a little.

Disregarding his amused expression, I passionately persisted, "But as time went on, nothing changed, things only got worse, trashier. *Debrie* is the most appropriate name for how I'm feeling right now."

"Oh, no," shaking his head decidedly. "This won't do."

His first recommendation was that I legally change my name, immediately. We spent the rest of the session considering name options that were suitable to the potential he saw in me. The two front-runners were *Estelle* and *Stella*, both of which mean *star*. I had always liked the name *Estelle* and soon *Estelle Joseph* became my new official legal name.

During these early sessions, I revealed that I once dreamt of becoming a professional dancer. I related the story about the day my mother caught me dancing, and how, during the beating that followed, she forced me to promise that I would never dance again. The doctor prescribed that I take a dance class immediately.

A few days later, I went to a midtown Manhattan school to enroll in a class. The live piano music drifting from one of the studios beckoned me. I peaked in and what I saw stole my breath away -dancers from varying age groups were moving gracefully to the music. The ladies were visions of royalty in their pink ballet slippers and tights, they were ballet princesses. The scene brought to mind my childhood desire of being a princess; here was my chance to play out my fairytale. So right there, I opted to begin my dance experience with a ballet class.

On the first day of ballet class, I was overcome by the freedom and beauty of dance. I couldn't believe I was actually standing in a dance studio and that there was absolutely nobody who could stop me from moving to the music. The movements of my body to the rhythm of the melody felt comfortable and familiar. For the first time, on that warm summer afternoon, I felt something stir in my chest area. It was my heart beating, and my spirit awakening. On that day, with the glorious sound of live piano music playing in the background, and the encouraging words of the dance instructor in my ear, my soul was reclaiming its true purpose. I was transformed! Standing at the ballet bar, a memory surfaced. A vague recollection of a time when I knew my true potential and all things were possible, and a little girl had promised herself, to never let anyone or any circumstance rob her of her joy and dreams.

Overwhelmed by my emotions, the tears rushed down my face. Embarrassed, I quietly gathered my belongings and made a quiet exit. But I returned the next day and every day after that. I had a lot of learning, catching up and dancing to do!

Deeper In the Murky Muck I Go

SO FAR, SO GOOD. Maybe there was something to that therapy mumbo-jumbo after all. My therapist's advice was working. My new name did make me feel better about myself, and dancing was giving me a glimpse into a world I had only dreamed possible. I felt more alive than ever before in my entire life. I was getting stronger mentally and physically. With those positive changes, I became even more committed to my therapy sessions and was letting down my guard and resistance, allowing myself to trust completely in his judgment and wisdom.

One afternoon, during the second month into treatment, I was lying on the couch with both arms behind my head, and shoes off. We were discussing how much I was enjoying dancing when suddenly my therapist extended his hand to me and asked, "If I were to give you this hand, what would you do with it?"

Without thinking, I took his hand and placed it on my right breast. Within seconds, I was undressed and my therapist was pleasuring me. I'd had pleasurable sex in the past, but for the first time, I had an orgasm, then multiple orgasms. I lay on the couch, for definitely more than our scheduled hour, doubled over in ongoing, intense waves of pleasure. He didn't undress. He only used his hands and tongue to please me. I had not been aware that a woman could have hours of orgasms.

After the session was over, my therapist simply eased his ample body out of his chair and left the room without a word, without any explanations, apologies or comments about what had just transpired. I lay there a while longer trying to compose myself, and dressed in a daze. I left his office, entered the elevator, drifted out the building, hailed a taxi, went home, and crawled into bed fully dressed.

The sexual relationship with my therapist continued for over a year, I continued to see him at least three times a week. We no longer had discussions about my past, my present, or my progress. The sessions were always the same, an hour of no talk, just sex. He never took off his clothes; I never touched him; nor did I ever see his private parts. I'm not sure if he received any pleasure from this, since I never saw evidence that he was aroused. It was not a give and take affair. I was the only one receiving. For once in my life, I didn't have to do anything but lay back, relax and enjoy. I took pleasure in the thought of receiving and not being obligated to reciprocate; that was deliciously arousing.

Throughout that year, I convinced myself that my therapist and I were in love. I conjured up an entire relationship. After all, whenever I told him that I loved him, he would respond with some version of "me too."

After all, I had evidence of his love for me. I knew that he was putting his reputation and practice at risk by having this relationship with me. And I loved him enough to promise myself that I would never reveal our secret to another living soul. Any whisper of impropriety could ruin him.

He gave me a private telephone number that I was to use whenever I needed him. When I left a message, he returned the call within a few minutes. He would call me at home on the days we didn't have a session, especially at bedtime, to tell me he was thinking of me. He would also call whenever he was away on business or on vacation with his lifelong female companion. I wondered if they had an arrangement or an open relationship. He'd returned with exotic gifts from his trips. He still had his radio program and dedicated songs to me, mostly jazz compositions by his favorite artist, John Coltrane. We both enjoyed Coltrane's rendition of *Blue Moon*, which was the doctor's first dedication to me. We exchanged gifts often and on special occasions, and celebrated with cake and wine. He even introduced me to his twenty-something adult adopted son. All of this transpired within the confines of his office walls. And I was paying almost three hundred bucks for each of our "dates."

Hypnotized by his power and charisma, I could not get enough. When in his presence, I did not want to waste a second of our time together in conversation. I just wanted the pleasurable feelings to commence immediately. He'd always begin by complimenting my outfit, which I always chose carefully. He would dim the lights and undress me slowly. He'd give me small kisses all over my face; but there was never any open mouth, or saliva exchange.

For a while, I accepted the strange, exciting situation as confirmation of his love. But deep down, I knew it was immoral. When I was alone, my Christian upbringing and mother's words would surface and fill my mind with constant self-judgment. Still, I was able to find a way to rationalize our behavior by telling myself that this was a unique situation, and only temporary. I convinced myself that we *were* in love and that's what truly mattered. And that we would somehow find a way to take our relationship outside his office walls, beyond the patient-doctor paradigm and make it "normal".

In the beginning, I never brought up the subject or demanded an explanation about the unnatural course our relationship had taken. I assumed he would eventually clarify. In moments of uncertainty, when I was alone, trying to make sense of it, I vacillated between the two possible reasons. First, he indeed loved me and was waiting for the right time, when I was "cured" to take the relationship to the next level. Second, what we were engaging in was some new form of therapy that was risky, but so effective that he was willing to put his reputation on the line so that I could get better sooner. As time when on, and I was still paying $275 per session for several sessions a week, with no discussion or change forthcoming. Moments of sanity started to set in through the fog of my orgasms.

One afternoon, I gathered the courage to demand an explanation. "What is going on here? What is this, some kind of relationship?"

Taken aback by the questions, he coughed a little while fishing for a reply, "You should learn to live in and enjoy the moment without concerns for the future. Estelle, just allow yourself to enjoy what's happening to you without judgments or reservations."

It was true. I was enjoying myself and I didn't want it to end. In that instant, I wanted his reasoning to make sense so I readily accepted his excuse.

Smilingly looking deep into my eyes, he said, "I have an idea that might help. You need to focus your energies on something besides yourself. You need to share this loving feeling. Why don't you adopt a pet?"

Not a bad idea since I had considered it before and thought it would be nice to have company at home, but my busy work schedule always kept me from committing.

"I've wanted to get a dog for a while. I think that's a great idea," I replied.

And as quickly as I had changed my name and enrolled in dance classes, once again I followed the wise old doctor's suggestion and found my way to a dog shelter to choose a new friend. A couple of days later, I had a white, shepherd mix, as my new companion. That evening, my therapist called to find out how we were doing. I was a nervous new mom, with a tiny, even more anxious puppy that would not stop yapping.

We discussed several name options and I finally selected *Bridges*. It was after choosing the name, I realized that this was a significant moment in my life. Instinctively, I knew that dog was about to transform my life in immeasurable ways. As I repeated the name Bridges, something stirred within me. Somehow, I knew he was the conduit capable of taking me from my current Hell to a better place.

Caring for a new puppy was an effective distraction and granted me some relief. The love of dance and my puppy's adoration were starting to dismantle the fortress around my heart. Being involved in the world and expression of dance was allowing me to shed layers of rigidity and repression. I was starting to learn self-love, and was softening up inside.

Bridges, with his innocence and playfulness, reminded me that there was some good in the world. No matter what mood I was in, no matter how weepy, mopey, or self-absorbed I got at times, he loved me. When he put his head on my lap, licked my face, or grabbed a toy to get me to play with him, he was letting me know that he was there for me. Bridges was teaching me what unconditional love was.

I was finally beginning to feel love. These awakenings were melting the walls of my heart, slowly cracking it open and causing me to crave human affection. I now wanted to share my life and new family, with the doctor, the man I was in love with. I wanted a normal life with the man I loved.

These realizations and my unfamiliarity with loving feelings, coupled with my therapist's contradictory ways, throw me into a deeper state of emotional mayhem. I was sinking deeper into the quicksand of overpowering despair.

The last time I felt that particular knot in my stomach was during the height of my struggle with my convoluted feelings towards my father. This doctor, like my father, did not care for me the way he was making me believe he did. The doctor's behavior was reopening the unhealed wounds of my father—the exact cause of my increased psychosomatic distress. I was becoming increasingly irrational and paranoid, and the secrecy was tormenting and driving me mad. My burden of shame, and self-loathing was unimaginable. I was Debrie all over again!

Declan knew I was going to therapy, and my therapist was that doctor on the radio that I listened to faithfully. "What's *really* going on?" He asked constantly with concern in his eyes and alarm in his voice.

I would answer with either, "Just old feelings coming up," or, "Oh, therapy stuff." Mostly, I would say, "Can't talk about it."

He must have figured more childhood stuff was surfacing, but baffled that I was not getting better, only worse. He was being as supportive as he could, but my "insanity" was adding a burden for him at work, more so, because he cared for but couldn't help me.

The few hours I was at dance gave me the brief escape I needed and helped me keep the ounce of sanity I had left. However, there were times when I was dancing that I could not get to that place of harmony with the music and dance. My thoughts would lead to him. After all, dancing was one of his first gifts to me.

This unpredictability made me angrier, more demanding, and needier with every passing day. I was becoming increasingly, unhinged. I would call his office insisting that I talk with him right away, no matter what he was doing. I would show up at the office without an appointment and demand to see him. Once allowed into his office, I was okay. I felt safe just being in his presence. But after about two months, that was no not enough. It certainly was not working for him either; I could tell he felt threatened. He had ended our sexual relationship when I began questioning the relationship, and I was feeling completely abandoned. Why had he stopped loving me? Wasn't I special anymore?

Now our sessions together consisted of my angry accusations about his abuse of power and threats of exposing him. He would sit silent during my rants. Then in an unflustered voice ask, "Did you get it all out of your system? Feel better now?"

No, I didn't. His silence and composure made me feel worse. He'd take on that doctor role and put me in my place—the patient's couch, unstable and delusional. In my delusion, I wondered, had I imagined or fantasized this entire relationship?

"Sweetheart, your feelings are normal. This happens a lot, Estelle. Often, patients fall in love with their therapists." The ultimate professional, he assured me that everything was fine and that we would get through this together.

My instability made me beg his forgiveness, apologizing repeatedly for my words and behavior, crying rivers of tears, proclaiming my undying love for him.

This escalated daily and it was clear he had a huge problem on his hands. He succumbed to suggesting medication. I was insulted, hurt, and devastated. I refused. His suggestion of medication made it clear that he thought of me only as a mentally unstable patient and that he did not love me anymore.

Since I refused medication, he emphasized that the only alternative then was for me to see another therapist immediately. He suggested someone outside of his practice, a female associate, who had a private practice in Connecticut. During my first two visits to Dr. Caroline in Connecticut, I just sat there and cried for the hour. On the third session, I talked only about my dancing and about my breakup with Dennis. Seeing that my therapist had called her personally, requesting that she see me as soon as possible as a favor to him, she knew that there was more going on than I was sharing. However, she allowed me space and time. I felt that if I opened up to her and revealed what was really bothering me, I would be betraying my love for the revered celebrity therapist.

At this point, I was in therapy every day of the week. I was traveling to Connecticut twice a week for my sessions with Dr. Caroline, while I was still seeing my regular therapist three times a week. It would take almost a month and the assurance that it was safe to trust Dr. Caroline before I opened up and tearfully divulged the true nature of the relationship between her colleague and me.

Although she tried her best to keep a straight professional face, I could tell that my confession shocked her. I could also tell that she did not initially believe me. I could see her surprise but her eyes told me that she thought I was nutty.

Upset by her reaction, I collected my belongings and said, "I can't believe this. You don't believe me, do you? You think I'm crazy and I'm making this all up!" She did not try to stop me as I said, "Thank you for your time," and rushed out the office.

Dr. Caroline called that night to apologize for making me feel like "I had not been heard" and suggested that I come in the next day so we could continue the interrupted session. I agreed to the emergency session. What else could I do? I had nowhere else to turn.

The next day, I relayed the story calmly and convincingly with enough details so she would take me seriously and believe me. I told her that he and I constantly exchanged gifts, spoke on the phone almost nightly, and expressed our love on a regular basis. I admitted that we only saw each other at the office during our scheduled appointments. But explained that seeing each other only at the office seemed logical to me because I though he wanted me to get better before we took our relationship public. After all my details and explanations, she realized I was not clinically crazy. But she needed final confirmation from the horse's mouth.

Can't Touch This

IN MY PRESENCE, DR. Caroline called my therapist on the phone. She relayed what I had confessed and asked, "Is she telling the truth?"

"You had a sexual relationship with her?" she shouted, eyes widen in disbelief.

He spoke for a while as she listened. He must have been using psycho-babble to justify his "special psychological treatment".

After a few minutes, she said, "I am not comfortable with this at all. The only way I can continue to treat and help Estelle is if you stop seeing her right away. I cannot help her if she continues to see you too."

He refused.

"Really?" she asked, again with an incredulous look on her face.

He said no again. I assumed he was probably explaining that it would be detrimental to my recovery if I stopped seeing him.

I could see she was appalled and confused. She abruptly ended their conversation with, "I can't be involved in this," and hung up the phone.

Visibly shaken, she slowly turned to face me and said, "I'm very sorry, Estelle, I can't help you."

The following day at our session, he greeted me with a proud smirk, "I can't believe she wants me to stop seeing you. I can't do that. You're my girl." My heart soared with delight. He still loves me my beloved was not ready to give up on me so soon.

That day, we did not engage in sexual activity, but that session felt more like the old days. I sat on his lap at his desk and we listened to music. Although I was enjoying our time together, I could not erase the reality of the situation. I could not brush aside Dr. Caroline's counsel. "It would be in both your interest to stay away from each other." Her reaction and the queasiness I felt from it had crystallized the unsanitary nature of our rela-tionship. I could no longer make excuses. Still, we had a nice afternoon together.

At the end of the session, he provided me the name and address of another female therapist. My first appointment was the following Monday afternoon at her Manhattan office.

I started seeing Dr. Cora, my new therapist, more often than him. This time, I told her immediately what had transpired between the old doc and me. She was prepared because she was able to react more unfazed than Dr. Caroline did. She didn't want to get into it and didn't ask for further details. He must have fed her a revised version; it was odd she had no reaction whatsoever.

Two weeks into my sessions with her, my old therapist became seriously ill, hospitalized and was to have a long recovery. This forced separation resulted in an abrupt weaning which was the best thing for that absurd relationship and me.

During that time I felt like a drug addict suffering from withdrawal. The emptiness his sudden absence created was a vulnerable and dangerous time. For any addict, trying to stay away from an obsession could lead to death because of the shock to the system. Since it does not recognize this new way of being, the body becomes confused and demands the old and familiar. That is why most people cannot stay drug free for long and revert or often advance to stronger substances. For me, my drug of choice was attachment to misery, suffering and my struggles I didn't know how to live without them. This new space gave me two choices. I could go back to living the way I knew, even take on new and more destructive relationships and behaviors, or hold on for the promising future I was starting to envision. Now, I had a Bridges a living being depending on me, helped me focus on the latter.

I told Dr. Cora my story. She helped me see how I was integrating learned patterns and mistakes of my past into my current relationships. She explained that since I was expecting my families' ungodly behaviors from everyone I met, and that's exactly what I end up getting. The experience with the doctor just reinforced that belief.

While I came to a better understanding of myself, I could not see how dredging the past was going to help me with my present mess. I was filled with "why this?" and "why that's" I could not understand why he had done what he did and why I had fallen for it. Why would a man in his position risk his reputation that way? How could I flush away my time, money, energy—into such a scenario? How could I be so stupid?

Although my shrink's method was not solving my immediate problem, to her credit, I discovered that we repeat so much of what we experience in childhood—good and bad—we seek out, and draw people and situations that are familiar, no matter how destructive or detrimental they might be to our well-being. Dr. Cora did not have answers for my current condition, and did not want to help me through it. So after two months, I left. I was starting to lose faith in the practice of therapy. The old doctor was unethical; Dr. Caroline simple washed her hands of the entire affair and did not report what she knew; and Dr. Cora was in denial that her colleague was causing his patients harm.

The old doctor's suggestions that I change my name, take up dance, and adopt a pet had merit, But, the nature of my past and the added damage he had caused was too traumatic to ever be repaired with minor fixes. My problems were equivalent to someone dying from a heart attack and requiring open-heart surgery only to receive band-aids by their physician. An ethical doctor would not recommend a band-aid for a patient who has received extensive stitches from open-heart surgery. Therapy works to a certain extent, but is not appropriate for everyone under every circumstance, and too often practiced in situations beyond its scope. There I was, needing a triple bypass, and these three charlatans were slapping band-aids all over me.

After I left Cora, I struggled on my own for a month. By now, I knew that therapy could not help me, but I figured it was better to talk to someone, anyone, about these feelings rather than keep them inside. In my anger, I was able to call the old doctor and ask him for a third recommendation. He owed me after all. Furthermore, I needed him to know that I was still having difficulties—more so because of his actions. Mostly, I wanted him to know that he could not just walk away from me so easily and ignore what he had done.

I traveled to Connecticut for six months to the new female therapist he suggested. This time, I was going to a therapist for a specific reason: to get it all off my chest. I talked about every member of my family and about what each one of them had done to me; I declared myself their victim. By then my anger towards the old doctor had turned to unadulterated revulsion—he had done me wrong and there was no way to justify his sick behavior.

I cannot say that the practice of therapy is useless, completely. There are decent therapists who help people. And to be fair, I did gain some benefits from my years on the couch. However, psychotherapy is not for everyone. If you choose to get counseling, be aware that some people can get addicted to having someone's undivided attention as they ceaselessly talk about their problems, without taking the next steps - making concrete changes. I have known people who have been in therapy for years and years and probably are still in therapy to this day. Therapy is not supposed to be a lifestyle but a transitory form of treatment. Be leery, as some practitioners treat their patients or clients as consumers and keep them dependent and coming back for more.

A Wasted Life, a Dream Unfulfilled?

RESENTMENT SATURATED MY WORLD, especially my dating life. The thought of being intimate with a man made me sick. My interest in sex was non-existent, for sex had betrayed me. If I hadn't been so blinded by my desires and orgasms, I would not have allowed myself the naive beliefs that had caused me this hurt. This hostility transcended into dance at an even deeper level and stole little by little, my love and joy of movement.

In an effort to take my dancing to a professional level, I started going to auditions. These experiences did not help improve my attitude though. No matter how hard I tried, no one hired me. The judges were kind, made encouraging comments on my natural abilities, and seemed genuinely impressed that I had been dancing for such a short time. However, the verdict was always the same: "Your technique is not strong enough," or, "We see gaps in your training. Try again later. Next!"

I would leave these tryouts filled with rage towards my mother. She had flatly denied me the chance and opportunity to achieve my destiny, my dream of being a dancer.

Furthering the frustration at these auditions, my heart filled with envy as I stood back to watch the more talented, gifted, younger dancers, who had danced and trained from childhood. I observed in awe as they twirled around the studio without missing a step of the routine, impressing the judges with their skill and performance. As I looked into their youthful faces, filled with hopes and aspirations, I regrettably concluded that I was at least fifteen years older than these dancers were, and knew that I could not compete.

So financially and emotionally broken, I reluctantly returned full-time to the irrigation company. With deeper sadness and confirmation that my mother's opinion was true, I accepted defeat. She was right all along: I never think before I act, I am a *jammet*, a slut who would end up being nothing more than just another unwed pregnant mother.

I returned to my sleep walking, dazed existence. This time I was a zombie with a bad attitude.

At the office, irritation seeped into all my interactions. I was mean and rude to employees and clients; no one could do anything right. As Declan grew increasingly impatient with me, we argued more. Who can blame him? I had not been a true business partner for some time. Our fights were getting so frequent that it was getting harder to contain within our private office walls. One Tuesday afternoon, after a particularly nasty fight in the presence of employees, I left work early to get away from the situation.

On my way to the bus, I had to stop for a drink. This was not the first time that had happened; it was becoming a habit. I also needed a drink or two at home to help me sleep. That afternoon, I sat at the bar staring into the drink, too upset to even take a sip. I looked around the pub at the other patrons and I did not like what I saw: hardened men, perhaps alcoholics who had probably been drinking since before noon. "Holy shit, I can't become one of these guys," I thought.

Wearily, I slipped off the bar stool, left my untouched drink, and made my way to my apartment and spent the rest of the evening in bed in a strange numbness.

My life had never felt so meaningless or empty. Then a chilling realization hit home. Tomorrow would be just like today and yesterday, and the up-coming days would only turn into the same sorry-ass month like all the previous months and years. That dreadful thought filled me with unspeakable terror. At first, my heart starting pounding, and then, I could actually feel my heart breaking. It was like the engine of a car. Finally seeing my reality for what it really was—sent the motor of my heart into overdrive. Then, it slowly started to fizzle and stall. I was dying.

So, for the first time in a very long time, I prayed. I did not get down on my knees or anything dramatic like that. I just sat on my unmade bed and in desperation cried, "God, if you're still up there, you gotta help me!"

As I said the words, I felt a calming relief. That uncomfortable oppressive gnawing pressure in my chest area lessened. I leaned back on my pillows and fell asleep.

Part II
Visions

TIPS TO HEAL BY

There's Power in the Spoken Word

Take a Trip— Inward

Give Yourself the Gift of Forgiveness

Family Matters, So Make Tough Choices

*Consider the Family Ties
That Continue To Bind You*

*Change is Possible When Yearned For
With Every Fiber of the Being*

Emotionally Healthy Children = A Peaceful World for All

*Look Back to Move Forward
& Find Your Forgotten Passion*

*Balance Yourself: Mix a Mental Activity
with Something Spiritual*

*Make Time to Connect To the Universe
It Is Our Greatest Teacher*

There's A Power in the Spoken Word

I AWOKE THE NEXT afternoon refreshed from sixteen hours of restful sleep. That customary tightening feeling I had around my heart and chest area had magically disappeared. I was lighter, freer. And for the first time, could breathe more easily!

The simple explanation would be I had gotten a few extra hours of much needed rest. The truth was something deeper and bigger than just sleep.

I believe the three critical actions I took the previous afternoon were influential in setting into motion that small, yet significant shift.

Stepping away from that drink and the bar, and deciding to choose a different path was the first. Seeking the assistance of a greater power was the next. By being humble and reaching out to God, I had acknowledged and accepted my human limitations. Finally, I was ready to admit my problems were beyond my capabilities. Most importantly, I had verbalized my appeal. Voicing my request somehow made me more responsible for whatever I was asking for. On that day, I became aware of the power of the spoken word.

When I first came to America, in conjunction with other aspirations, I had academic goals as well. Suddenly, I started noticing catalogs and advertisements for events taking place at local universities.

I started taking yoga on my lunch break, which helped get me through the workday in a saner fashion. In yoga class, I noticed people who seemed calm and together, their life seemed more meaningful somehow. They often talked about being on a spiritual path. I craved the peace they exuded. They happily shared their knowledge, and invited me to accompany them to various workshops and seminars taking place around the city.

Soon, I was attending workshops and lectures almost every weekend. I soaked it all in. Like a shipwrecked woman rescued and offered life- saving food and water, I relished it. From these lectures, not only did I learn that my past was just that, in the past and I had no control over it—then or now —and in order to move on, I had to make peace with it. And that gaining control over my present would be a good place to start. I understood that not getting the love I needed, as a child does not mean I am unlovable. It was imperative that I believe it. I could lavish myself with the love I wished I had received early on.

Setting aside quiet, alone time during my day to reflect inward, a sort of checking in with my-self was an effective start. This withdrawal from the external over-stimulation of daily living calmed my overactive mind. Like a parent sitting on the sidelines, observing their child at play, it was during those still moments that I was able to notice my pessimistic thought patterns and worked on changing them. I discovered the power of aroma and color therapy. I was amazed at how a whiff of pleasing scent or splash of color could uplift the mental and emotional state. These small practices weren't an instant cure however; they set me on a more centered optimistic path. Besides, it sure beats grabbing a drink to dull the pain.

In 2006, I was accepted at New York University's International Relations program. Now I had to consider the facts: I had not been in a classroom for almost twenty years, along with exhaustion from my many years of working, not to mention my recent psychological roller-coaster. I concluded that I would not be successful juggling the responsibilities of running a business and attending an academically demanding college. As I was not happy or interested in what I was doing at work, it seemed natural, and the perfect time to give up my partnership in the irrigation business to attend school full-time. So I did. And that's how and when my new life of understanding myself, my ancestors, and the world around was born.

Take a Trip Inward

WITH MY PRAYERS ANSWERED, my days were now brimming with newfound motivation. For the first time, I was excited about life and living. Immersing myself in my studies, I was surprised to find I enjoyed being a student. Moreover, since I had always enjoyed traveling, I took advantage of the academic traveling opportunities the school provided. My favorite professor, Antonio Rutigliano, who taught medieval and classical studies, led that program.

I gravitated towards Professor Rutigliano's classes because of his fatherly mannerisms. He treated all his students—teens and adults alike—as his children. At the end of class one day, after he read my paper aloud, he handed it back and whispered, "You have talent, kid." I swelled with pride.

While on one of our class trips to Italy, at lunch I was stuffed from eating a large plate of the best spaghetti and meat sauce I had ever tasted. I could not eat another bite. The professor had chosen that particular restaurant because he wanted the class to experience "the best cannoli in the world!" I was full and do not have much of a sweet tooth, so I turned down the dessert. The professor wasn't having any of it. "Estelle, you have not lived until you've tasted this cannoli!" He said this as he opened my mouth and shoved the pastry in. He was absolutely right!

The day we landed in Italy, the sweet-toothed professor took us up hills and valleys without telling us where we were going. We moaned the whole way, wondering what we'd gotten ourselves into, all he would say was, "It will all be worth it!" Upon reaching our destination, we were greeted by a wonderful ice-cream parlor, where everything was fresh and homemade. He treated us to two scoops of the best gelato in all of Italy! With every lick, I raved about how "this was the best thing I've ever tasted." Realizing how much I was enjoying myself, the professor secretly got me an extra scoop of coconut gelato. I tried rejecting the third scoop, but he held firm and reminded me that I "might not have the chance to enjoy anything like this again."

A required reading for one of his courses was Dante's *The Divine Comedy*. That book had a profound impact. This three-part epic poem was written in the 1300s during the last nine years of Dante's life, while in exile from his native Florence. Dante was embroiled in political and religious turmoil. He was coming to grips with the recognition that his life had been meaningless and that he was simply suffering the consequences of his actions and decisions. Dante was betrayed by everyone, including the church he had served faithfully most of his life. At a completely hopeless point in his life, with nowhere to turn, he took a trip inward, into himself, into his psyche. In today's modern civilization, Dante's experiences might be construed as a serious case of a midlife crisis or a mental break. My interpretation was, sometimes you have to have a breakdown before you can experience a breakthrough.

In his journeys as a pilgrim, Dante travels through Inferno, Purgatory, and finally Paradisio. Only allowed to enter paradise after he has learned certain lessons, come to a better understanding of himself and has a change of heart. Dante's trip is quite torturous. But luckily, he is blessed with guides along the way who help lead him to and through his new understanding and awareness. One of Dante's guides is Virgil, a Roman poet whose writings were influential in shaping Dante's philosophical view of the world. The poem's theme is clear: Dante hopes to lead readers to a better understanding of their role in the universe, and help prepare them for a new and more purpose-driven life.

What touched me most about this story was how much I could relate to Dante's plight. Like the poet, I had come to a juncture in my life where I was alone and afraid. I wanted and needed a change. I too had reached a point in my life where I had nothing left to lose and no other place to go but within. In seeking that conversion, I came to realize that I was in possession of the answers to my many life questions. The avenue to creating the life I craved, and the path to understanding and establishing my own paradisio on earth resides within me. I too encountered many guides along my journey to lend a supporting hand. Dante had Virgil, and I had many including dear Professor Rutigliano.

My studies served their function, for as the scales of ignorance fell I began to view the world with new eyes. I can now see how amazing our universe truly is. My studies also brought me to a new understanding of ancient civilizations and the immense contributions of the African people. The knowledge of their achievements initiated within me a new sense of pride and need to succeed. That appreciation was instrumental in propelling me onward when faced with academic challenges that made me faint-hearted.

My college years also taught me the causes, and negative domino effect of historical occurrences that shaped our world. I learned how slavery and colonization were exploit as tools, to keep people—even families within societies—divided. This mentality would play out in family dynamics and in their behaviors towards each other. These morals were mirrored and handed down from generation to generation. I discovered how a society's inhabitants relate and treat each other within the communal and familial setting often determined by tradition, and religious beliefs. As I studied these patterns, I understood my own family's conduct more clearly. While I will never excuse my family's upbringing, I have come to acknowledge the factors in motion.

My father and his siblings inherited their alcoholism from their parents. Today, society is aware that alcoholism is a disease, but then, it was not treated as such. Fortunately, none of us inherited our father's alcoholism, but did not escape catching his violent streak and our mother's feeble disposition. After all, a rotten tree can never produce good fruits. I know what I'm made of, and when I look to both sides of my family tree, what I see scares me.

In the case of my mother, violence surrounded her. Her greatest difficulty, I believe, was not having control over her own body and the number of children she bore, thus creating a greater dependency on her lunatic husband. On and off for about twenty years, my mother was barefoot and with child, and in constant fear for her life. Today, we know the effects hormones and pregnancy have on a woman's body and state of mind. We also know about post-partum depression. My mother never had time to rest, be aware of her true feelings, or recover physically or emotionally. We can all agree that childbearing under those circumstances would be extremely rough on anyone.

I firmly believe that my mother's hostility towards me stemmed from exhaustion and feeling overwhelmed by her pitiful life. The question then remains; why did my mother stay with my father? Back when I was little and asked my mother that question, I could not grasp her rationale. Today, I have a better understanding of her motivations. Before my mother's conversion to Pentecostalism, she was a practicing Catholic. One of the few doctrines the two religions have in common is their stand on morality and sex. No matter what religion she belonged to, my mother was bond by a decency code. She would have been condemned if she dared engage in sexual activity with anyone other than her husband.

Some scholars believed that those in positions of authority invented religion as a means of controlling the masses. Even as a teen, I sensed that my mother's preacher was taking advantage of the poor people in his congregation. Their blind faith made them vulnerable, keeping them in a state of obedient pacification. Nineteenth century German philosopher, historian, and political theorist, Karl Marx referred to religion as the "opium of the people."

My mother was a concrete example of this. I understood her position, even though I still can't condone her actions and decisions. I was able to identify with her desperation, and need to seek redemption. I could see how she could get tunnel vision in her devotion and zeal to secure her place in heaven. My mother, of all people, needed the escape that her religion provided. She needed her opium of salvation and hope for a better afterlife.

My travels helped defined and ground this new knowledge, especially in countries with ancient history: Egypt, India, Peru and Greece. In these sacred places, my spirit awakened. I gained insight into the differences between religion and spirituality. When I think of *religion* words such as *dogma* and *allegiance* also comes to mind. To me, religion is a stagnant set of beliefs and rules with no flexibility for spiritual growth. It is like a clan, with group thinking and values. Spirituality, on the other hand, has no labels: Christian, Jew, Pentecostal, and so forth, it's purely "I am, therefore, we are." It is the awareness that within this universe there is no separation, for we are connected every single one of us, to each other and to a divine source. Within that interconnectedness, is an individual consciousness that allows a person to evolve as their understanding of themselves and the world around them grows. An individual practice or journey filled with love and appreciation for all of life. It is love and compassion practiced not for riches and glory in a life after death, but acceptance of oneself and others in the present, here and now.

Understanding this is what helped me differentiate between the uncompromising customs of the religion I experienced as a child, and my current spiritual practice.

Give Yourself the Gift of Forgiveness

IN DECEMBER 2002, AT the age of eighty-four, my father died a wretched, lonely man in his dilapidated shed in Saint Lucia. I felt little emotion when Francisca called with the news, it was as if a family acquaintance had died, and not the man who gave me life. I also found out that, during the final years of his life, my mother took care of him.

It wasn't easy, but I decided not to attend his funeral. I concluded that attending meant I was participating in the celebration of his life. Since there had not been an occasion for celebration during his lifetime, it would have been a meaningless sham to pretend his life had meaning. Ironically, some of my siblings (the same ones who discussed plots to kill our father in the past) found my actions disrespectful and mean-spirited. It didn't matter to me what they thought, because I felt comfortable with my decision, as I do today.

I no longer permit the opinion of others to influence me or my life. I no longer force myself to have an affiliation with anyone who does not respect, or treat me with dignity, even those who share my genes. I am closer to the siblings who have an interest in sharing a life free of our old ways. Some are not, and so I have chosen to eliminate them from my life. This was not an easy decision for me by any means.

Even though I had emotionally disconnected from certain siblings, the bond between us was inescapable. The depth and intensity of our family malfunction made our attachment tight, making it very difficult to detangle from its many tentacles.

As children, we knew we were a strange bunch, so we became fiercely protective of each other from outsiders who tried to take advantage of us due to our precarious circumstances. Like prisoners, forced to protect each other from their jail warden and the criticism of the outside world, but at the same time, had no problem turning on their fellow inmate. During the course of trying to escape our prison gang, I realized my breakout would be thornier than I first imagined, and had to come up with a radical plan.

I acknowledged that, although I was making the choice not to have relations with some of my siblings, my feelings and memories of them would always remain. Whether I was eliminating or adjusting these relationships,

I had to reconcile my feelings towards each one of them. Realizing that even when people are no longer physically in your life, the power of unsettled emotions keeps you bound to them even accumulating additional acrimony. In addition, when that disconnection occurs in anger or strife, it does not lead to healing. It is only when the healing balm of forgiveness is applied, that the letting go of disturbing connections becomes possible.

As a teenager, I didn't know about the possibility of being able to remove oneself from their past and not continue in the cycle of abnormality. But the one thing I knew for sure was that my father could not be a part of my life.

As a child, I thought death was the only way he'd be out of our lives. The manner in which he threatened everyone—constantly reminding my mother that she'd be dead before she could leave him, alarming us with his machete-wielding antics—it was clear death might be the only way this family contract could be dissolved.

Is it not strange that for a long time I could say I loved my father, but cannot say the same about my mother? Of all the outlandish stunts my father pulled, none caused me the level of hurt, or personal physical and emotional pain my mother caused. At least I have memories of my father's tenderness towards me. Still, I chose to separate from him but not from my mother. In my heart, I know that my mother's actions stemmed from my father's years of victimization. My father was an evil man and my mother was responding and reacting to his actions, trying to survive the best way she could. I learned nothing good from having known my father, but I learned from my mother.

My relationship with my mother is blanketed in—and made possible by —the mighty forces of forgiveness. With forgiveness comes acceptance, and so I have what I consider an accepting relationship with my mother.

I accepted the fact that she will never understand who I am, and that ended my need to seek her approval. Regardless, my mother did teach me my most valuable lessons: always look to God, for only by grace are all things possible, and to have an unwavering belief and faith in God's divine love and wisdom. These teachings have sustained me, it is what kept me afloat on the turbulent seas of my life and for this; I will always be grateful to her.

No matter what, my mother unyieldingly expressed her faith and gratitude to God through songs of praise and prayer. The hymns I heard her sing in her misery, with tears in her eyes, have proven instrumental in my life today. I sing these songs of worship in moments of challenge and triumph—for their words still hold true to the woman I've become. This is my favorite hymn I learned it from my mother.

All to Jesus, I surrender.
All to Him, I freely give.
I will ever love and trust Him,
In His presence daily live.
I surrender all, I surrender all.
All to thee my blessed savior, I surrender all.

I no longer try to ignore the pain my family caused me, especially my mother. Forgetting is impossible, but I had to forgive for my survival and sanity. Forgiving them was a gift I gave to myself, and boy, did I have some serious forgiving to do. Before I could be in a position to forgive anyone, I had to first, let go of the self-hatred I had towards young Esther for not being the perfect child, or teenager, and forgive the adult Estelle for continuing her imperfect ways. Forgiveness I discovered is an act of great courage that generates and speeds up all healing processes. Included in this progression, is the honesty factor. Being truthful with oneself and family members is imperative.

What illuminated this insight was when I thought of, and focused on, one of the greatest lessons from the great master Jesus. While being crucified, moments before dying, he prayed for his persecutors with these words: "Father, forgive them, for they know not what they do."

If Jesus can forgive the most unforgivable act, forgiving anything else seems entirely possible. Like vitamins or a curative ointment, I take my doses and apply forgiveness daily.

Family Matters, So Make Tough Choices

I HAVE GAINED NEW perspectives on families that are as unique and complicated as families themselves all over this globe. In certain households, the family unit is placed above the individuals who make it up. These people set aside their dreams and desires, and keep in accordance with the interests of the whole—the family and head of the group. Parents make important decisions, especially career and marital choices for their adult children. But what happens to these individuals, or the parts of that whole, as they relinquish their universal right to a life of purpose and passion for the wishes of others?

I wanted to dance professionally, but according to my mother, along with being sinful, that was not a respectable line of work for a woman. So, that enthusiasm was stifled until, I decided to make it part of my life. By the time I had gathered the courage to pursue dance it was too late. My saving grace however, is that today I can dance whenever I want, and experience that joy on a personal level.

Without the zeal that springs from having personal and emotional freedom, what happens to a person's soul, their essence? Anyone living an unfulfilled life endures that feeling of incompleteness day after day. For me, it was a strange physical sensation that felt like a heaviness, yet a vacant hole inside. When ignored, this emptiness often develops into physical pain, which can cause serious illness and even death. In my case, the disturbing symptoms manifested as chest and abdomen discomfort that resulted in surgery below my navel area. Like the empty belly of a starving person, with hunger comes the frantic need to fill that need. When not satisfied with life-affirming elements, that hole will end up being filled with unhealthy vices and activities, which renders you ineffective to those who depend on you.

The safety instructions given on flights by airlines, comes to mind—the one where passengers are warned that in case of an emergency, they should first secure their own oxygen masks before attempting to assist others with theirs. The reasoning behind this instruction is that if a person is not awake or conscious, then he or she is not capable of being of service to others. Some people, focused on assisting others forget to put on their own life-sustaining oxygen masks becoming dizzy or unconscious in the process. In other words, take the time to be health and whole so you can be available and able to support those who need you, especially your family.

A family unit should not be a group of people cohabitating or interacting purely for biological or legal reasons. If a group considers themselves family but does not respect or like each other, then there is no family. If you are in an environment that causes you suffering it is your duty to save yourself and the young ones in your charge. I assure you, whatever is going on in your home; your children are learning that behavior. It is not safe or sensible to remain in such a situation. Sadly, it is what most people do.

The family institution is not unlike the human body. When just a small part is diseased, the entire body suffers and cannot work efficiently. I am not referring to the occasional disruption of a head or toothache; these disturbances are normal and expected, and in a healthy body, easily alleviated. Just like in families, it is natural to have sporadic flare-ups and the occasional discord.

However, some family relationships, such as mine, are a more debilitating kind of sickness, not unlike a cancer, that eats away at all the healthy parts. In such an instance, a more radical resolution, amputation or chemotherapy, is required. The act of cutting off a body part or detaching from a family member is never easy and might seem excessive; however, the severing of a draining extremity, or rather a unconstructive family relation, might be the only way to bring healing to the rest of the body or family unit.

There may be some who already have a gut feeling that this drastic action is necessary, still they can't do it. Instead, they hung on to their infected limb or relationship at all cost. Maybe out of fear of looking different or being alone, sometimes looking like a family or like everyone else give folks a sense of normalcy. Whatever the reason, when it comes to the family, it is imperative to disregard how things look on the outside, and focus solely on what is really going on.

I am not assuming that people everywhere are living miserable lives. If you have a loving, caring family then you are lucky and blessed, and my heart rejoices with you. However, many others accepted their families as a cross they have no alternative but to bear. Remember, you have options. The decision to continue to remain a part of a family that does not elevate you is also a valid choice. But, if you are weary from carrying the load weighting you, then give yourself permission to lay it down.

This takes audacity, but above all, it is your God-given right to a life purposed on *yourown* individual dreams and aspirations.

Consider the Family Ties That Continue to Bind You

WHILE SOME RELATIONSHIPS WITH time and effort can be improved, there are others, giving up is the best choice. The key is in differentiating between these when deciding how to proceed. However, do not allow that decision-making process to become an added burden. Go unwaveringly with your instincts and true feelings.

If after speaking or interacting with a family member, you feel spent and your sense of self plummets, that is a flashing neon sign indicating that there needs to be a shift. Another signal of a troubled relationship is the party's inability to be honest. If you find yourself discussing the problem with everyone else but the person you are having the issue with, that situation needs addressing. Do not deal with these family concerns in a roundabout way, but frankly and at the source. Any other technique will only escalate the drama you are trying to circumvent.

If as an adult you are still intimidated by your parents or siblings so much so that you can't express your feelings to them directly, then chances are you will hold on to your feelings of resentment and impose it on those you deem weaker, or take that inability to stand up for your self into the other areas of your life. So, if your relationship with your parents is not what you wish it, the problem stems from the way they related to each other as husband and wife or treated you as a child. Their actions have adversely affected your emotional development, and has created the person you are, and don't necessarily like.

If growing up, we learned that relationships are based on fear and criticism then these are the ingredient we would take into or magnetize in our new relationships, especially romantic ones. We all know that relationships based on these qualities are doomed, and just add more misery to our lives. More complexities arise when, while still trying to deal with the effects of our past, and struggling with problematic relationship with our parents; we are also bringing new people and their issues into the mix. Inevitability, we find ourselves involved in a complicated hot-potato juggling act as we try to keep it together. We try unsuccessfully to keep all those potatoes in the air. But we can only do that for so long. Soon we become exhausted from it all, as these burdensome relationships overpower us. Before long, we are standing in a mess of smashed, soiled potatoes. If we choose not to address problems with our parents and siblings they will continue the same dense patterns of behavior that always bothered us. They only sting and hurt us more today. Since we haven't been honest with them, they probably don't appreciate how their words and actions still affect us. Their words and behaviors have so much power over us, that we may even find ourselves reverting to a childlike state, feeling, acting, even talking as we did when we were children.

This biological link is a thread, as strong and innate as the umbilical cord, which keeps us tied emotionally, not only to our mothers, but to our entire family. That connection is undeniable and near impossible to break or alter. But we can make modifications to ensure that everyone involved is getting the nurturing needed, unless we do so, these interactions will continue to frustrate and bring much distress into our world. No relationship magnifies the type of affiliation we had with our family more than our romantic ones. From who we choose, or avoid marrying, to the problems that plague, or the conduct that nourish our current relationships. Save making a conscious effort at change, we will become our parents, or fancy people like them.

Take a moment to think about your most recent relationship, what did you like or disliked about it? Then examine the parallels between that relationship and the one you had, or are having with your family. You will find connections and similarity between the dysfunction or function of your childhood with what is going on with your relationships in the present. Striking isn't it?

If, after several attempts at discussing your concerns with your family, they refuse to listen, obviously, you won't get the validation you need to mend. Every time they react this way, they are repeating the same old message you heard all your life: your feelings do not matter. In such an instance, you might have little choice but to walk away. There comes a point in life when you have to decide which battles are worth fighting and which ones are not. For me, my family dynamic was fractured on so many levels I had no choice but eliminate some of them, lessening the weight and complications.

Walking away from a relationship does not always mean a permanent break though. When you have given yourself emotional time, you can always allow people back in to share your redesigned self and life. Choose wisely. This time, let it be on your own terms. You will discover that as you bring them in from a place of love and truthfulness, your relationships will be healthy and rewarding.

Change Is Possible When Yearned With Every Fiber of the Being

BREAKING FREE OF MY shackles of pain and self-destruction has not been easy, but my commitment to their annihilation has been real and steadfast. I became determined to building my own little heaven on earth, whatever the cost.

My first glimmer of salvation came when, out of desperation, I reached out to a God I had stopped believing in, and had turned my back on. I thought that he, like everyone else, did not care. Just as the reasons for my suffering were multifaceted, so was my path to healing and wholeness. Redemption does not come in a one-size-fits-all package, but must be a more custom-tailored exit from the strangling hold of the dreadfulness of our past and present. Travel and relationship changes were part of the course that offered me the most intensive healing. However, these were costly actions that might not be right or easily accessible to everyone.

Rest assured though, that there are many routes home. Choose an approach, if that one does not produce the results you seek, try another, and then another. Believe that your deliverance draweth near. Keep your eyes, heart, and mind open. Small steps, taken one day at a time, will produce tangible and life-transforming results.

I know that stepping out of the darkness of your past and into the brighter possibilities of your future is as difficult as it sounds, but you can do this. You, as I once was, are now at a crossroads. The life you have imagined is within reach. It is possible. We were all born with an inextinguishable flame or light within us, it is what keeps our yearning alive and will see us through to our liberation. I offer no quick fixes, just a solemn promise. If you make the commitment to walk in that light, you will be guided by it and never again walk alone.

In my most trying moments, I know without a scintilla of doubt, that I was lifted and sustained by the mighty, forgiving hand of my God. It matters not, what you call Him: Jesus, Yahweh, Allah or Jehovah. It is important that you believe in something greater than your mortal self. The fact that I am here today alive, sober and intact, is a testament to powers not my own. What I had though, was a profound belief in something. For a while, I did not know what that something was, but *it* knew me. I know that *it* is available to you too, if only you believe.

Those of us who have childhood trauma view the world differently. Our experiences left us feeling separated from our God-given purity, joy and completeness bequeath to us at birth. It was replaced with vulnerabilities and insecurities which make a child's survival instinct go into overdrive. In order to protect ourselves we take on defensive, combative personalities. Aspects we deem stronger and better able to do battle with whomever or whatever our scary situation was. In trying to shield and defend ourselves, we become that negative aggressive self. We doggingly hold on to it at all cost. As adults, we keep that fighting spirit alive, forgetting that this is not who we truly are. Every time we make use of that false identity, we feel more alienated from our Divine self. The truth is though we can never truly be separated from our Godliness. You the fantastic Being, created in the image and likeness of God is still in there. Just a little lost, buried under layers of disillusion and distrust, and still operating in protection mode.

Now that we are grown and physically away from the old hurtful environment or family condition, we can no longer hang on to the childlike survival methods we used back then, it no longer serves us. We've at a place where we must fully engage the world and live in it. We cannot escape it. Pursuing our protective techniques of the past adds to the dysfunction that hunts, haunts, and handicaps us. If we had the strength as children to build those walls, we have twice the strength as adults to bring them down. As President Reagan said in reference to the Berlin Wall, "It's time to tear down that wall!" We have power beyond measure to break down any barrier that prevents us from seeing and being our true omnipotent potential.

This process works best when the war plan is "whatever it takes" and your mission statement does not include the word *but*. Deliverance in any fashion can only manifest when yearned for with every fiber of the being.

Accepting and understanding that our current experiences are manifestations of the lessons learned in childhood, is critical. If you do not believe that these lessons, instructive or destructive, play a role in your current life circumstances, then the strategies I speak of may be of no use to you. There are reasons behind everything we do, the choices we make, the actions we take, and the manner in which we react to any given situation. These decisions are not made in a vacuum. From the person we decide to marry, the way we raise our children, to the kind of food we buy at the grocery store - all are influenced by what we have learned as children.

Trying to make these life-alterations without the recognition of how subliminal and deep-seated the reasons for our deeds and conduct, would be akin to attempting to plant a beautiful garden in an area filled with weeds. For a while, the newly planted foliage would seem fine, and might even thrive for a time. Until the stronger, more dominant weeds take over and choke the fragile plants. Until nothing remains of your promising garden except a more fortified weed patch. To successfully eliminate weeds or what you no longer want in your life, they must be yanked or destroyed entirely from the origin—the roots. You are precious, so yank gently, but persistently. In order to give your new way of life a fighting chance, you must start your planting phase with weed-free soil, a clean slate. Please remember that a quick remedy is not an honest and effective way to tackle problems. No matter how ugly or weedy your truth, you'll have to face it, since it's your reality.

The first step in moving forward might be to look back and find the child you lost along the way. What were your childhood aspirations before you got so busy with life and protecting yourself? Re-examining this childhood longing could reveal much regarding your present discontent. The fact that it will not disappear from your memory indicates that there is unfinished business. Do you still have the "wish I had" feeling? It could be for a musical instrument, photography, drawing, or anything else you once felt passion. It is never too late to pursue dreams. Exploring this longing can bring you closure or open you to a new trajectory. This could be an initial step towards opening a door that leads to healing.

Giving yourself balance is helpful. If you decide to engage in a plan that entails mental energy—psychotherapy or academics, balance it with something physical. Swimming, jogging, and walking can serve as an offset. Add spirituality in the mix - attend religious services, practice meditation, or yoga.

If there is a place—another country, a particular beach, or mountain area—that calls to you or comes up often in conversation, then it's a sign you should not ignore. Make that trip and find out. You might not choose to go globe trotting as I did, but traveling and moving yourself from one place to another, even for a short time, offers rewards.

Finally, vow wholeheartedly to yourself that you have had it with your current state of affairs and warrant much more. Make that your prayer. Say it aloud and voice your request. That allows you to take it outside yourself and seek assistance beyond your human abilities. You don't need to attach reasons, justifications, or judgments to it. You crave a life of abundance and fulfillment - that is reason enough. Focus on your heart's longing for a specific period—a week, a month, or whatever timeline you can feasibly commit. When that stage is over, you no longer make your prayer a request, but turn your attention to being thankful. For the same length of time you prayed, you now fill your heart with appreciation, as if you have already received your blessing. You are no longer in an asking, but grateful frame of mind. Be grateful to the universe for clearing your path, showing you the way, and filling your heart with the courage and fortitude necessary as you walk the rocky road that will eventually lead to your new world. Every great achievement begins with an intention, and is sealed with gratitude.

Think of your emotional body as a computer. The accumulation of old files and outdated programs will cause your computer to operate in a sluggish and uncooperative manner. It is susceptible to viruses, which may cause it to crash. In order for your computer to work at its optimum, you must attend to those old programs and replace them with updated versions and virus protection. Sometimes you may even need a completely new operating system. There must be a letting go of the past in order to fully embrace and engage the present. Deprogram your mind from its erroneous, cynical belief systems and reprogramming it with a new, superior way of thinking and operating. With this new mindset, we can restart our lives, fully charged with clear awareness. This time around, we are the informed parent, or whoever, bestowing onto ourselves the compassion we wished had been shown to us.

With your new outlook, life is easier. You discover you have gained wisdom and have talents you never dreamed possible. You'll also find you are more forgiving of yourself and of others, not as judgmental of your fellow-man or women as you once were. You become aware that they too are on a path and might be struggling with the same obstacles you once faced or still present a challenge. You now have a new appreciation for yourself because you know how gallant you had to be in order to arrive at the place you are today.

With your newfound wisdom, you comprehend that, although your heart might go out to others, you no longer have the need to get personally involved in their troubles. You may offer words of encouragement or a supportive ear with a loving, open heart. It takes practice, but when your heart is open, listening without judgment, condemnation or preconceived notions, becomes possible. You now recognize that an individual's journey is an ongoing process, which we all have to tackle on our own and in our own way and time—no one can do it for us.

This bears repeating. This isn't easy and not for the faint of heart. The good news though is, no matter what the problem, or how impossible things may seem, we can break free of the past that threatens our present if we really want to. And when we do, we will emerge victorious because we stand and act on the solid foundation of love—for ourselves and others.

All the answers we need are within us. The human soul is created with untold wisdom. Intuitively, we'll know how to cure our ailments if we take the time and effort to look and listen inward. When we choose bliss, our world becomes filled to overflowing with abundant possibilities. It is truly magical.

We will experience life in amazing new ways. Imagine you've been a slave in a palace to a mighty king for many years, and one day there's a discovery that you are the only heir to the king's fortune. All along, the fortune was yours but you were not aware of it. Thoughts of elation are only possible by the discovery and knowledge. Now we have the understanding of what it was to once be lacking or struggling and now be on the other side, enjoying abundance. We have a fuller appreciation for our newfound wealth. This simple example does not do justice to the fulfillment that emotional wholeness brings. It is truly an indescribable way of being.

Of course, you will still be confronted with the daily stressors of life. However, you are now equipped to navigate them, and their effects will not be as distressing or long lasting.

When the difficulties of living life threaten to overwhelm me today, I am secure in the knowledge that I am safe, and I know how to bring back my equilibrium. In learning and discovering about myself, I have found what I need and the ways to keep myself grounded and centered. I can steer and find my way back to inner calm and peace.

Dancing has always offered me that calm and freedom, and still works for me. I put on a piece of music and move my body to the beat. When I move my body, I shift my state of mind. I'm instantly soothed. In the moment of freely swaying my body, my heart fills with an overwhelming sense of gratitude, a feeling that overpowers and replaces any feelings of self-pity, want, or lack of whatever I think is missing in my life.

In discovering yourself, you will find your own grounding mechanisms. You will find your special place of solace and serenity. You will find what makes *you* feel at home.

Emotionally Healthy Children = A Peaceful World For All

LIKE MY MOTHER, MANY other parents believe it is their duty and right to spank their children to discipline them. It is their responsibility they believe, and rightly so, to teach them that negative actions and behaviors have consequences, misdeeds will be punished, and obedience is required above all else.

These are all noble and valuable instructions parents are trying to teach. However, are these lessons the only ones children learn while pain and humiliation are inflicted upon them? Every time a parent hits a child, he or she is also teaching that it's acceptable to lash out, especially at those who are weaker, smaller, and can't fight back. The child is learning that violence is a suitable response to anger and frustration. Children who are beaten discover that those who claim to love, and obligated to protect them, are the ones who cause them the most pain. This teaches them to fear, rather than respect their parents and other authority figures. That fear translates in different ways - hostility and bullying have escalated greatly in schools in recent years.

When abused by a grown-up, no matter the words uttered by that person, the child hears a variation of the following: "I can hurt you and there's nothing you can do about it", instilling in that child deep feelings of powerlessness. Some parents actually believe that an explained spanking makes it better. It does not, and only serves to confuse the child further by the parent's contradictions. "Honey I am hitting you to teach you that hitting another is wrong" or "I am causing you this pain because I love, want to protect you and know what's best for you." Since that child is not feeling love, but pain, it stands to reason that, they will learn to accept that love hurts.

One thing I am certain of, my mother had options and could have done better. There were other disciplinary measures she could have chosen other than trying to beat the badness out of me. Other less violent and degrading methods would have taught me lessons and garnered results.

If for example, you do not like the fruits from a tree planted in your garden, you do not spend much time wondering what is wrong with the fruit, but instead try to find the problem with the tree. You might till and fertilize the soil, trim and cut its branches and even do a little research on the history of the struggling tree. The fruit is just a by-product of the tree.

Likewise, children's behavior is usually a reflection of what is going on in a home; any tensions or conflict between parents—the tree—or family members or relatives—the branches, will adversely affect children's actions and reactions creating insecurities that cause them to act out or retreat in fear. It is impossible for children to behave when their life is in upheaval.

Parents need to allow their lives, and not just their words, to reflect the kind of person they want their children to become. During the first several years, children are thick sponges, and ready to absorb everything exposed to them. So impressionable, they have the ability to learn languages, musical instruments, and other things that happen to be more difficult as they get older. This is the time for parents to become the artists and sculptors of their children's lives. They have the opportunity to color and shape them into productive, law-abiding, fulfilled adults. If a parent's life has been an honest and consistent example, then a solid foundation has been set, and they find that the human structure they have to work with is more malleable and easier to mold.

Children adulate their parents, for that reason parents should be open, readily admitting their own imperfections to growing children. By being honest, parents can avoid appearing hypocritical when their past errors come to light. This minimizes feelings of resentment, often demonstrated as rebellion. Children believe it unfair that while they are punished for their mistakes, parents do not seem to face any consequences of their own.

While there are certain rules that may not be practical in application to both adults and children, others should be set fairly. One rule that could be appropriate for everyone is the words used in the home. When an adult curses or uses derogatory words in the home, it is unrealistic to think their child will not use them as well. Punishing a child for something learned directly from the parents is a way of setting two different sets of rules. It is extremely important that parent be proper examples for their children. Again, be who you want your children to grow to be.

Parents should show mercy. Being merciful does not mean you are being inconsistent in your discipline, but rather showing a rare moment of genuine forgiveness, tempered with self-control. The more egregious the infraction, the more effective the act of mercy will be, for leniency touches and inflects the heart of any wrongdoer, especially a child's. It is an opportunity for them to experience what compassion and forgiveness is all about.

Spanking as discipline is really an attempt at a quick fix, usually done in anger. If drumming on a child were an effective disciplinary tool, parents would only have to do it once or twice. Having to spank repeatedly is an indication that this technique is not working. No matter how out of control or wild the child may be considered, a beating is never an effective way to get their attention, obedience or respect. I assure you spanking will only add to the problems and make matters worse.

One type of punishment does not work for every child. The form of discipline used will be more effective when it corresponds with a child's particular temperament. Discovering what works best takes effort and forethought on the parent's part. It is time and energy worth investing, since it will produce better results than the alternative. Being a parent is challenging, but it is important to acknowledge and remember that being a child is not easy either.

I am not particularly interested in the physiology of abuse, that important aspect I leave to others.Just as a mechanic does not concerned themselves with the automobile accident, but chooses instead to focus on the repairs. By buffing out the scrapes and dents and getting the engine running smoothly again, the technician gets the driver back behind the wheel and on to the business of living. Likewise, I do not burden myself too much with what or why, an abuser abuses but rather choose to concentrate my energies on aiding those who have been abused and are grappling with its annihilative aftermath. I will say, however, that I do believe all forms of abuse are about power and control. Nothing makes a person feel better about themselves then beating on someone smaller and weaker who cannot fight back.

Parents' causing their children anguish is the worst kind of abuse. Although, it is equally despicable when a stranger hurts a child, in church, school or on the streets, at least a child knows that they can get away from there and be safe at home. But, when the abuse is in the home that child has nowhere to run. Not feeling safe at home is the most awful feeling in the world.

I do not presume to have all the answers. Nevertheless, I speak from the perspective of a teenager, who while growing into adulthood, spent much time in inquisitive observation pondering this decision. Even then, I concluded that I was not suited for parenthood, and my position became more solidified as I grew into womanhood. This was mainly my way of ending the cycle. I could not overlook the glaring truth that I was not equipped for motherhood. Knowing I could not trade my hereditary or learned behaviors, I was not about to take a chance on ruining an innocent life.

My mother's dedication to not "spare the rod and spoil the child" was not for my benefit or best interest. She reckoned her own lack of power by overpowering me. I recognize that there are other parents, who enthusiastically join her refrain in reciting this well-known and too-often quoted biblical passage from the Book of Proverbs. Their rationalization for causing their children agony is after all, for the child's good. I have often wondered whether the rod these proponents refer to is the same "rod and staff" that the Psalm says will, "comfort and prepare a table before me" and every other child of God who believes. Can this rod be an instrument that accomplishes two separate and opposing tasks, console and demoralize? Most people would agree that in Jesus' day, the staff was a Sheppard's most valued tool, used to guide their flock. I can't imagine a good Sheppard using his staff to club his sheep into obedience, can you? May I suggest in that scripture, Jesus was instructing parents to make use of their staff the way a fine Sheppard would, to gently guide their tender human flock onto the righteous path.

I would also like to share words from the gospel of Matthew: "Therefore all things whatsoever ye would that men should do to you, do ye even so to them" (Matthew 7:12 KJV). It is not my intention to swap or interpret Bible verses; that would be a futile exercise. What I am hoping to point out is that many Bible passages have a corresponding balancing text that teaches another way to go about the same issue. Regardless, I can't reconcile the idea that a God who said, "Suffer the little children to come unto me, for theirs is the kingdom of heaven" (Matthew 19:14 KJV). And, "Except ye be converted, and become as little children, ye shall not enter into the kingdom of heaven" (Matthew 18:3 KJV), would advocate causing children such suffering by beating them with sticks. The only explanation that makes sense to me is there are other interpretations parents should take into consideration, given the era that Bible verse was written. Either way, I know that beating anyone or anything—except maybe a rug—never resolves a thing.

How would it feel if the tables were turned? You've aged, too old and feeble to care for yourself, and are now in the care of your children. I will make a simpler prediction, like my toothless grandmother made to my father: "They will treat you the way you've treated them." Whatever stage in the life cycle, childhood or adulthood, we all deserve to live in love and dignity. Remember, you reap what you sow; therefore, violence breeds violence and compassion breeds' compassion.

My circumstances were certainly extreme, and yours may be more or less so. However, no matter the degree of violence - the consequences are the same. If you are one of the many adults whose childhood experiences included aggression, I beg of you, please take the time to examine your life and break free of those past ties that still bind you.

Adults still controlled by their unresolved pasts, see the world as an unsafe place. They live with a "them against me" mentality and their actions and decisions are involuntarily root in and motivated by that belief. Imagine the future of the world if the emotional conditioning of its inhabitants, are being maturated in abuse. These children someday soon will be in decision-making and governmental positions. What kind of country and world would we have if a victim of cruelty became president of the United States? Considering the immense responsibilities and powers given to that person, and how their decisions have the capability to shape the world, shouldn't their psyche be free of emotional clutter that hinders decision-making and reasoning abilities? That emotional freedom, or lack of it, will determine how they engage the world, whether it's through peaceful and humanitarian means, or conflict.

***

Can you see how abuse has many levels and appearances, and extends beyond the individual and family unit? Cultures can be cruel as well. It is no accident that we are such aggressive societies, for it is individuals within families that establish practices and ideals that create cultures. Our children observe and learn the lessons of how the strong dominate the weak; men belittle women physically and emotionally because they deem them less relevant. Boys develop into their fathers and girls reflections of their mothers. Even in western cultures, boys and girls are reared differently. Boys are taught that they are superior and therefore expected to take on leadership roles, while young girls are trained to aim their expectations lower and that there are certain vocations they cannot or not allowed to pursue or succeed at by nature of being female.

We continue to condone and accept these different manifestations of maltreatment, as we look the other way. Governments do the same to their own people in the name of cultural preservation. There are nations all over the world that, because of cultural beliefs, deny some of their citizens' personal liberties by nature of their sex, race, tribe, or caste. We rationalize these actions as private family matters or a nation's sovereign right.

Individuals who have experienced abuse and emotional turmoil themselves most likely perpetuate these social traditions. And because their hearts are hardened by their pain, they've converted into ruthless thugs who easily rise to positions of power, enabling and continuing these barbaric ways of life. They keep the cycle of demeaning and doing harm to the weak and defenseless going strong.

Untold psychological damage persists, as adults, like infants, are not permitted to make decisions or govern their lives. They are told who to marry and what occupations to have, choosing these and other life affirming pleasures are privileges they'll never enjoy. In certain cultures, a man is allowed to have as many wives as he pleases, while the woman are not even permitted to have a say in who her one and only husband will be. Grave consequences befall a woman, including losing her life, if she is even suspected of any impropriety. These human beings are shunned, publicly beaten, mutilated, or even killed when they rebel or break these cultural norms, with no power over their futures and destinies, their survival is a hopeless one.

Parents who abuse their offspring mar not only them but their descendants too, while governments and cultures have the ability to exploit and ruin entire generations of families. The outcome is the same: People are learning and living violence. It's all connected, and we are all interconnected in this global family.

Every human deserves the right to practice his or her freewill. When lovingly guided and instructed on how to make informed choices, children will use their freewill to improve their lives and the world around them and adults must have the autonomy to lead a life of their own making. When denied this right, there is abuse. We must start looking out for our families, both local and universal. Refusal puts us all at risk as the future of humanity depends on it.

This may seem like the wishful imagines of a dreamer. Then please join me in my vision. The task may appear daunting and the goal seemingly impossible to attain. But I know a more harmonious world is possible. Since individuals make up families, and families create communities that mushrooms into societies, the survival of our cultures depends on the mental and emotional wellbeing of its citizens. And it is up to us, each individual, to ensure that we have wholesome families and, communities. Kindness begins at home, with the children. When families interact lovingly and humanely, cultures will begin emulating those qualities. Then our world will have a chance of becoming more diplomatic and unified.

Make Time To Connect To The Universe. It Is Our Greatest Teacher

WHILE IN ITALY ON a trip with my class in 2008, as we waited at the entrance of a museum, a group of noisy, excited children, who seemed like first graders, marched passed us. Like my class, the children were waiting for their entrance tickets. To keep them occupied, one of their teachers led them in a chorus of counting backwards from one hundred, skipping every other number. My class and I stood there stunned as we watched and listened to the children easily count backwards. At first, I felt amazement, then pride and joy, then envy. My heart filled with resentment, because in that moment, I wished I were one of those kids at the start of my life. I wished that I had, at that age, been lucky enough to have had experienced what those children were so casually enjoying.

Then, I realized that I was indeed enjoying exactly what those children were enjoying, and that age didn't matter. I was there now. I was going to see the same great pieces of art too, and I was in a lovely, exciting new country. More importantly, I had the eyes and heart of a child. This opportunity was a great blessing, and I am indeed a lucky woman.

A few months later with some of those classmates, I stood on the shores of Sicily and looked towards Africa. We were considering how amazing it would be to just cross a bridge (if there was one) or walk on water, and be in another continent in minutes.

It had never dawned on me that people could sleepwalk through their lives, and it was in Italy that I first realized I had been doing just that, sleepwalking through mine. It was while walking through Saint Francis Assisi's garden at his home in Tuscany, now a shrine, that I first felt his powerful yet peaceful presence. The experience was so surprising, intense, and real that I could not keep silent. I burst into uncontainable tears. My group and professor thought I was having an exhaustion meltdown. As I sobbed, my bewildered professor begged for an explanation. "Please tell me what the problem is, so I can fix it!" he pleaded, but I could not. I had no idea what was happening. To dodge their baffled whispers and looks of concern, I drifted a short distance and sat alone on a stone, but I was not really alone. I took a few deep composing breaths as I relaxed in Saint Francis's presence. There in his company, I vowed to awaken, and live my life by his gentle example. I quietly said: *Hi, my name is Esther, Brie, Debrie, Estelle Joseph. I've been sleepwalking through my life, but no more. This has been my wake-up call!*

As I stood in wonder one morning on the massive stone remains of Machu Picchu, it was apparent that giants or a great people had once been here. As I stood in their footsteps on the mountains, the idea of forgiveness saturated my consciousness. I became fully aware of my abilities to move mountains as well. Peru was where I was touched by, and fully able to internalize, the true power of forgiveness. It was there that I finally understood the difference between my past failed attempts at intellectualizing forgiveness, or idle repetition of catch phrases, "you should just forgive," and the true concept and reality of what forgiveness is really all about. It was a letting go, or surrendering that infused my entire being—mind, body, and soul, and I felt physically lighter for it. The weight of years of sadness and anger just fell away, like an old garment I no longer needed. It was then that I made the determination that healing, without forgiveness, is not possible.

In India, what touched my heart the most was the Golden Temple. I like to call it my Golden City. People from all over India and the world come here on pilgrimages. This complex, built around a temple on water, provides its visitors with basic services to keep them comfortable while on their religious journey. No one is turned away; instead, they are welcome to stay as long as they wish.

While at the Golden Temple, pilgrims are served three healthy, hot meals, cooked on the premises. Also provided, is an area where individuals or families could rest or sleep, with bathroom facilities. Some people stay for days or months to offer their prayers. This special place is safe and protected, and upon your arrival, you get the feeling that you are entering a holy city. While visiting, our group learned that the place operates entirely by volunteers and the goodwill of donors, and is completely free to visitors. This is a place of community and deep love for humanity. Everyone was treated equally—no one was Indian, no one was American, and no one was a tourist. We were all part of the same human race. Everyone—especially the volunteer worker—was compassionate and dedicated to creating a comfortable and safe environment.

My heart and spirit were touched and moved beyond any expectations I could have ever imagined. I was inspired to give more of myself, and be a better, more loving human being. To me, aspiring to greater and higher states is what life should be about. It's certainly what the person I've grown into is continuously striving to do.

It was during a beautiful sunrise boat ride on the sacred Ganges River, that I made the greatest discovery of all. Love was patiently waiting for me in India. It was there that the final pebble rolled away from my heart and I became completely exposed, like a newborn babe. On that river, I came face to face with unconditional love from the one person that I had been searching for all my life. I met her, took a long look, and liked what I saw. It was me—flaws and all—that I finally discovered, and embraced. I finally grasped that, above all, I had to love me!

Later, that same year, I was on a pilgrimage in Egypt. Because of his governmental connections, our Egyptian guide was able to get my group private time in the King's Chamber at the Great Pyramid. That is a big deal! And our Egyptian guide, Mohammed, reminded us over and over again that this was a once in a lifetime opportunity. Such access costs lots of money, and is usually allowed only to the rich and famous.

Once within the Pyramid, we had to crouch up a long, very narrow, dark and dusty passageway to the room called the King's Chamber. It was difficult and dangerous, and some from the group chose not make the climb. I, on the other hand, could not wait to get there. In the room is a sarcophagus, an ancient tomb. Each member of my group had the privilege and honor of lying in the sarcophagus built centuries ago by the amazing people who erected that marvelous monument. Before getting into the coffin, where kings and pharaohs probably once laid, I once again had the opportunity to marvel at how far I'd come.

It was then I realized the enormity of my healing process, the tedious and grueling work that had been involved, and still lay ahead. Suddenly my experience took on an extraordinary and hard to explain turn. It felt like fragments from an authentic, superior me were being magnetized or drawn back to an empty or shell-like me. Like a broken humpty-dumpty I was being patched back together again by unseen hands. I felt the weight and clutches of my past and all the dreadful experiences ease effortlessly away. I lay in that tomb, wailing from the shock and relief as renewed energy surged through my body. I floated out the Kings Chamber and the Pyramid a different person. It was then I started tapping into my inner higher power, as I became aware of the unlimited and universal resources available to me. I can't possibility explain these experiences. I can only say that as I visited each country, I was retrieving parts, or bits of myself, that had been waiting for me to reclaim. As I received and embraced those aspects of myself, I was restored.

My mother was right about one thing: I am different. It took me a while to acknowledge and admit that I do not have to live my life like everyone else. I am as much, or even more of, a spiritual than physical being. I came to understand that my spirituality is the glue that keeps the other areas of my life together. In order to keep my spiritual center vibrant, I must nourish it as much as the other parts of me. That focus on balance is what keeps me centered.

I had taken my first yoga class years before as an aspiring dancer. But in 2007 my love affair with yoga became a serious commitment. I adore and practice yoga and meditation daily. A combination of Vinyasa and Kundalini yoga practice gives me emotional and spiritual stability. Although I love all styles of yoga, my passion lies in Kundalini, one of the oldest forms of yoga. It fosters every part of who I am, and helps me achieve oneness with myself, and the universe.

Over the years, I have become involved in other forms of energy work, including Reiki and crystal healings. But to me, the purest form of healing energy is located in the earth's energy power spots. These grids are electro-magnetic pulsations buried within the earth, and it surfaces similar to how underground water surfaces to form a spring. The difference is water is visible, while energy is experienced. These energy centers provide me with tremendous soul and emotional rejuvenation. Much like the way a battery needs recharging, so do I. When I am thrown off kilter, a visit to any of these sacred locations is the best way for me to get super-charged back into balance. Visits to sacred locations provide wonderful healing opportunities. In the spirit of sharing these healing opportunities with others, I would like to combine my love for travel and spirituality, by some day serving as a spiritual travel guide.

Amazing things happen to me when I travel, I become my best self. I enjoy being in one place one day and a completely different one the next. I am at home wherever I am, no matter the country, city, or state. As a child, I didn't feel at home in my house, so I sought refuge in my mind's eye and willed it to take me to places I could only dream of.

Today, I continue to dream, but now I have the power to make my dreams a reality. I dare to go wherever my mind, cash, and line of credit will take me.

My life is an adventure, a constant journey. I've traveled with groups and by myself. It does not matter whether I'm on my own or with company, I am never alone. I connect to people wherever I go; conversation flows easily between us. My new friends are as intrigued by me, as I am by them. When I travel, I naturally meld with all people and places. I adopt and embrace my universal family.

Today I live in my heart, within that rediscovered and refurbished space where my inextinguishable fire burns. The beauty of my home is that I can take it with me wherever I go, and make necessary improvements and adjustments along the way. Transmutations are made every moment of every day. As I make certain that the doors and windows of my inner sanctuary remain open and inviting, the more my love and joy for life and others grow. When I am at home and content within, I am able to feel my connection to all of life—every plant, insect and human. This unity and oneness of being is my natural state and birthright.

I covet a world that is free and safe for all. It is my prayer, that the freedom to find and reclaim your individual promise land becomes your reality. That is your legacy.

13.95

7/15/13.

LONGWOOD PUBLIC LIBRARY
800 Middle Country Road
Middle Island, NY 11953
(631) 924-6400
mylpl.net

LIBRARY HOURS

Monday-Friday	9:30 a.m. - 9:00 p.m.
Saturday	9:30 a.m. - 5:00 p.m.
Sunday (Sept-June)	1:00 p.m. - 5:00 p.m.

20092720R00103

Made in the USA
Charleston, SC
27 June 2013